LUTHER'S AUGUSTINIAN THEOLOGY OF THE CROSS

Augustine teaches the Scriptures to Martin Luther (by Paula Kuiper).

LUTHER'S AUGUSTINIAN THEOLOGY OF THE CROSS

The Augustinianism of Martin Luther's
Heidelberg Disputation and the Origins
of Modern Philosophy of Religion

Marco Barone

Foreword by David J. Engelsma

RESOURCE *Publications* · Eugene, Oregon

LUTHER'S AUGUSTINIAN THEOLOGY OF THE CROSS
The Augustinianism of Martin Luther's Heidelberg Disputation and the Origins of
Modern Philosophy of Religion

Resource Publications
An Imprint of Wipf and Stock Publishers
199 W. 8th Ave., Suite 3
Eugene, OR 97401

www.wipfandstock.com

PAPERBACK ISBN: 978-1-55635-599-8
HARDCOVER ISBN: 978-1-4982-8675-6
EBOOK ISBN: 978-1-4982-3589-1

Manufactured in the U.S.A.   05/30/17

To my Lord and Savior, Jesus Christ.

"For the preaching of the cross is to them that perish foolishness; but unto us which are saved it is the power of God. For it is written, I will destroy the wisdom of the wise, and will bring to nothing the understanding of the prudent. Where is the wise? where is the scribe? where is the disputer of this world? hath not God made foolish the wisdom of this world? For after that in the wisdom of God the world by wisdom knew not God, it pleased God by the foolishness of preaching to save them that believe. For the Jews require a sign, and the Greeks seek after wisdom: but we preach Christ crucified, unto the Jews a stumblingblock, and unto the Greeks foolishness; but unto them which are called, both Jews and Greeks, Christ the power of God, and the wisdom of God. Because the foolishness of God is wiser than men; and the weakness of God is stronger than men . . . God hath chosen the foolish things of the world to confound the wise; and God hath chosen the weak things of the world to confound the things which are mighty; and base things of the world, and things which are despised, hath God chosen, yea, and things which are not, to bring to nought things that are: that no flesh should glory in his presence. But of him are ye in Christ Jesus, who of God is made unto us wisdom, and righteousness, and sanctification, and redemption: that, according as it is written, He that glorieth, let him glory in the Lord."

1 COR 1:18–31.

CONTENTS

FOREWORD

BARONE'S BOOK IS A superb and convincing treatment of a grand subject: the faithfulness of Martin Luther to the theology of Augustine in proclaiming a radical gospel of grace, founded on what Luther called "the theology of the cross," in contrast to the heretical "theology of glory." In setting forth the gospel confessed by Luther, Barone works with the Reformer's *Heidelberg Disputation*, unfortunately long overshadowed by his Ninety-Five Theses.

The scholarly examination of the theology both of Luther and of Augustine is at the same time a powerful, if implicit, call to twenty-first century Protestantism and to Roman Catholics to test their confessions against the theology of the Protestant Reformer and of the church father.

Playing off the readiness of both Luther and Augustine to present their theologies as Christian philosophy, the book concludes with a demonstration that the theology of Luther and Augustine exposes modern philosophy, particularly that of Leibniz and of Kant, but by implication all of modern philosophy. The axiom of Luther that every philosophy that takes unaided reason as its origin and authoritative rule will be Pelagian in nature and content is shown to be true in the philosophy of these two towering, influential thinkers.

In light of the commitment of much of Protestantism today and of the Roman Catholic Church to a "theology of glory" and in light of the rule of reason over all of philosophy, especially in the schools, it is not to be wondered at that the religion of most of the Western world is Pelagianism. Here is a reasoned defense of the "theology of the cross."

David J. Engelsma
Professor Emeritus of Theology
Protestant Reformed Seminary
Grand Rapids, Michigan

ACKNOWLEDGEMENTS

THERE ARE SEVERAL PEOPLE to whom I am indebted. Dr. Catherine Kavanagh, not only for her essential academic guidance, but also for her patience and understanding. My parents, Francesco and Rosanna, for their constant support and encouragement through the years, and my brothers, Vincenzo and Andrea. My friends Martyn and Manuel, for their support (especially Martyn), but, above all, for their friendship. The Limerick Reformed Fellowship: this congregation has given me in three years much more than I will ever be able to give to it in all my life. Paula, for her encouragement and enthusiasm. Above all, my heavenly Father and my Lord Jesus Christ who loved me and gave Himself for me, for making me understand that glory comes through the cross.

INTRODUCTION

THE IDEA OF THIS book was born of a combination of two factors. The
first was the study of the theology of Martin Luther. This study consisted
in a close reading of a number of the German Reformer's most important
works. However, in the course of the relatively long pilgrimage along which
Luther was accompanying me, I was followed by another friend who did
not immediately make his presence known. I refer to Augustine of Hippo.
Proceeding in my reading journey, as I tried to introduce Augustine to
Luther, I discovered that it was not necessary. In fact, the German reformer already knew the African Bishop rather well. Even more surprisingly,
I observed how Augustine got along very well with Luther. Therefore, I
decided to enrich my study of Luther with the reading of Augustine. It
reached the point where I was silent during almost the entirety of our
journey, and I left the two giants talking while I listened and contemplated
the points of agreement and disagreement between the two. This agreement was particularly evident on four theological issues: free will, virtue,
righteousness, and the cross.

This fascinating journey surpassed a merely theological interest.
This is the second element that encouraged me to write this present work.
Luther's works created in me a particular interest for an interesting philosophical thesis that I think can be implicitly but with good reason deduced
from Luther's thinking. This concept is that, when man relies only or
mostly on his "reason" in his study of theology, the theoretical outcome is
always a man-centered, or auto-soteriological, form of religion. To express
it another way, when Luther's theology of the cross and its foundational
Augustinian theology of absolute grace are entirely or partially denied,
the consequence is always some form of Pelagian theology, which Luther

xiii

would call the theology of glory. Thus, I started to think that this was a topic worth pursuing. Moreover, the agreement between Augustine and Luther on the aforementioned theological topics could give substantial authoritative support to the Lutheran philosophical thesis I mentioned above. In light of my knowledge of the mainstream philosophy or religion of the modern age, the aforementioned idea appealed to me. However, I decided to study further the philosophy of religion of two of the most representative philosophers of the modern period, namely, Gottfried Wilhelm von Leibniz and Immanel Kant. I did this in order to verify Luther's idea, which I like to call the 'antitheticality' of the philosophy of the cross. The conclusions that I have reached are basically in harmony with Luther's intellectual prediction.

Dropping the metaphor, to summarize, the idea for this book was born during the simultaneous study of Augustine of Hippo and Martin Luther which I conducted through a close comparative reading of their main works. This research was of both theological and philosophical interest. In fact, the outcomes of both aspects of my study are contained in the present work. Concerning the theological side, as I read Lutheran works, such us *Lectures on Romans, Heidelberg Disputation* and *The Bondage of the Will*, Luther's extensive use of Augustinian works caught my attention. It was the reading of Luther's *Heidelberg Disputation* that particularly encouraged me to study the Augustinian nature of Luther's thinking. This is because this *manifesto* of Luther's theology was intended to be an *Augustinian* disputation among a group of *Augustinian* intellectuals. This means that Luther presented his theses as *Augustinian*. Thus, chapter 1 provides some introductory information regarding the historical and theoretical background which is necessary in order to engage in the study of the Augustinianism of the message of Luther which I have called the philosophy of the cross.

The 28 theses which constitute Luther's *Heidelberg Disputation* can be divided into four thematic groups: 1) theses 1–12, the issue of good works and virtue; 2) theses 13–18, the freedom of the will; 3) theses 19–24, the theology of the cross and the theology of glory; 4) theses 25–28, righteousness. However, I have changed the order of the theses because I think that, in this way, the reader will gain a better understanding of Luther's Augustinian position. Therefore, this will be the division: 1) theses 13–18, the freedom of the will; 2) theses 1–12, the issue of good works and virtue; 3) theses 25–28, righteousness; 4) theses 19–24, the cross. Chapters 2, 3, 4, and 5 are dedicated to the aforementioned theological issues respectively.

The aim of these chapters is to display the substantial presence of Augustine in Luther's *Heidelberg Disputation*, to demonstrate the essential agreement between Augustine and Luther on the points in dispute, and, therefore, to prove that Luther was accurate in asserting that his theses were solidly grounded on the authority of the famous church father.

Chapter 6 is the philosophical conclusion of my dissertation. The theological exposition of the previous chapters, besides demonstrating the Augustinianism of Luther's *Heidelberg Disputation*, is instrumental in giving to Luther's philosophical thesis a solid authoritative basis. Grounded in these chapters, the closing chapter aims to explain and to substantiate Luther's thesis concerning the "antitheticality" of the cross. In this section, I have expounded the theological conclusions reached in Kant's *Religion Within the Boundary of Pure Reason* and of Leibniz' *Theodicy*. I did this in order to compare these conclusions with the conclusions of Luther's intellectual adversaries: Pelagianism and Semi-Pelagianism (among which Luther includes Scholasticism). I have demonstrated that the positions of both Kant and Leibniz contain a theology which is essentially Pelagian. Now, according to Luther's philosophical thesis, every theological system which ascribes most or all the authoritative priority to man's reason tends inevitably to a Pelagian theology, that is, to a theology antithetical to Luther's philosophy of the cross and, consequently, in opposition to Augustine's theology of absolute grace. Therefore, I have argued that Luther's Augustinian thesis is proved by two of the most important and influential representatives of philosophy in the modern age.

The philosophical and theological conclusions of this research, coupled with their development, do not claim to be comprehensive and definitive. However, I believe their accuracy has been sufficiently demonstrated and I hope that these outcomes may foster further study in the same direction. With respect to this last point, the closing paragraph of chapter 6 briefly explains in what sense Luther's philosophical concept may be helpful for philosophical research, especially in the fields of philosophy of religion and ethics. I have now presented the aim of my book with its methodology and its anticipated outcomes. I conclude this introduction with the hope that my modest contribution has gained the approval of my travelling companions who "being dead yet speak"[1] and who, for which I will never be sufficiently thankful, have loudly spoken to me, and continue to do so.

---

1. Heb 11:4.

CHAPTER 1

PREMISES TO
THE *HEIDELBERG DISPUTATION*

THE LIFE AND WORK of Martin Luther can be described as a continual disputation. His position of professor and doctor of theology often compelled him to be a public disputant. Luther fits very well into Peter Cantor's ideal description of this specific part of the work of a doctor of theology of the late medieval age: "The disputation is the wall of this structure of study: in fact, nothing can be properly understood, nor faithfully preached, if it is not firstly chewed by the tooth of the dispute."[1]

The disputations that Luther wrote and attended are essential elements for a thorough understanding of the development of his thought. In fact, the Lutheran[2] writing which is unanimously considered the most famous is a disputation: I am referring to the *Ninety-five Theses*, in Latin called originally *Disputatio pro declaratione virtutis indulgentiarum*. This

---

1. "In tribus igitur consistit exercitium Sacrae Scripturae: circa lectionem, disputationem er predicationem. Culibet istorum mater oblivionis et noverea memoriae est nimia prolixitas. Lectio autem est quasi fondamentum, et substratorium sequenium; quia per aem eaeterae utilitates comparunt. *Disputatio quasi paries est in hoc exercitio et aedificio; quia nihil plene intelligitur, fideliterve praedicatur, nisi prius dente disputationis frangatur.* Predicatio vero, cui subserviunt priora, quasi tectum est legens fideles ab aestu, et turbine vitiorum. Post lectionem igitur sacrae Scrupturae, et dubitabilium, per disputa ionem, inquisitionem, et non prius, praedicandum est; ut sic cortina cortinam trabar, et caetera." Cantor, *Verbum Adbreviatum*, 1.1.2. Emphasis added.

2. With "Lutheran" I mean "according to Martin Luther." I do not intend to speak for the Lutheran church. This is true here and every time the reader will find this term.

1

text turned Luther's existence into a disputation not only in the academy, but also in his own daily life. This work has a fundamental place in the research of every scholar of Luther. However, from the point of view of their contents, the *Ninety-five Theses*, with few exceptions,[3] cannot be compared with the others main works of the German thinker.[4] This disputation is not even the best piece of theology among the Lutheran writings of the same category. The earlier *On the Power and Will of Man Apart from Grace* (*Questio de viribus et voluntate hominis sine gratia disputata*, September, 25, 1516) and *Disputation Against Scholastic Theology* (*Disputatio contra scholasticam theologiam*, September, 4, 1517), and the subsequent *Heidelberg Disputation* (*Disputatio Heidelbergae Habita*, April, 25, 1518) address matters that in the *Ninety-five Theses* are mentioned only vaguely and that Luther will later call "the real thing . . . the essential issue" in contrast with the "trifles" of "Papacy, purgatory, indulgences"[5] and similar matters.

In particular, the *Heidelberg Disputation* has become the manifesto of Luther's thinking inasmuch as it contains the hallmarks of his entire theology.[6] First of all, this work addresses topics which are vitally important not only for theology as such, but also for philosophy: good works, free will, the revelation of God (i.e., the antithesis between the theology of glory and the theology of the cross), and righteousness. Secondly, in

3. See, for example, the last four theses: "92. Away, then, with all those prophets who say to the people of Christ, 'Peace, peace,' and there is no peace! 93. Blessed be all those prophets who say to the people of Christ, "Cross, cross," and there is no cross! 94. Christians are to be exhorted that they be diligent in following Christ, their Head, through penalties, deaths, and hell; 95. And thus be confident of entering into heaven rather through many tribulations, than through the assurance of peace." Luther, *Works of Martin Luther*, 29–38.

4. On August 1518, Luther will comment on his own theses in the work entitled *Resolution on the Dispute Regarding the Value of Indulgences* (*Resolutiones disputationum de Indulgentiarum virtute*). This work is very important for understanding the position that Luther had at that time. Moreover, this work allows the reader to appreciate more the *Nienty-five Theses*, mainly because the author explains them according to the theology of the cross that he had presented and defended at Heidelberg in April of the same year.

5. "I give you [Erasmus] hearty praise and commendation on this further account—that you alone, in contrast with all others, have attacked the real thing, that is, the essential issue. You have not wearied me with those extraneous issues about the Papacy, purgatory, indulgences and such like—trifles, rather than issues—in respect of which almost all to date have sought my blood (though without success); you, and you alone, have seen the hinge on which all turns, and aimed for the vital spot. For that I heartily thank you; for it is more gratifying to me to deal with this issue, insofar as time and leisure permit me to do so." Luther, *The Bondage of the Will*, 319.

6. This point has been abundantly proved by von Loewenich, *Luther's Theology of the Cross*.

discussing these topics, Luther is able to set forth not only a distinctive theology, but also a certain hermeneutical key by which to interpret those philosophies which are not based on revelation. Luther would call them "theologies of glory." Moreover, and most importantly for the goal of the present work, Luther appeals to an authority whom to consider decisive is an understatement: "... these theological paradoxes ... have been deduced well or poorly ... from St. Paul ... and also from St. Augustine, his most trustworthy interpreter."[7]

The aim of the first part of this book is to display the Augustinian basis that Luther himself attaches to his *Heidelberg Disputation*. These theses are one of the manifestos of Luther's thinking and of the thought of the Protestant Reformation, and their decisive Augustinian spirit will be shown. Secondly, against the background of some of the most important and representative philosophies of religion of the modern age, the present work will seek to demonstrate the accuracy of Luther's claim which is especially present in theses 19–24: all those systems of thought which either do not start from, or reject, or do not properly consider the incarnate and crucified Logos, i.e., Jesus Christ, end by revealing themselves as moralistic philosophies which try to reach God by mere human works. In other words, all these philosophies share a common intellectual and theological Pelagian foundation. This is the Lutheran philosophical thesis which we will deduce from our study of the Augustinianism of Luther's paradoxes. We will dedicate the second part of this thesis, that is, chapter 6 to the discussion of this concept against the background of three giants of philosophy, namely, Aristotle, Leibniz, and Kant.

In order to introduce the *Heidelberg Disputation*, we will analyze the short premises that Luther himself gives right before the Theological Theses themselves. In fact, here are very concise but significant indications that point to the occasion and nature of this book. We will adopt the same procedure for the treatment of the 28 Theses in the following chapters. Before focusing on them, it will help for a better understanding of our subject to begin with some introductory data.

> Brother Martin Luther, Master of Sacred Theology, will preside, and Brother Leonhard Beyer, Master of Arts and Philosophy, will defend the following theses before the Augustinians of this renowned city of Heidelberg in the customary place, on April 26th 1518.[8]

7. Luther, *Heidelberg*, Second Preface.

8. *Ivi.*

By "before the Augustinians," Luther is referring to the General Chapter of the German Augustinians. As is quite well known, on July 2, 1505 Martin Luther, at that time a young and very promising student of Law, was almost killed by lightning while he was on the way to Erfurt where he intended to spend his academic leave. Terrified, Luther made a vow to saint Anne, the patron saint of miners (the profession of his father), promising her that he would become a monk if she saved his life. On July 17 of the same year, a very young Luther entered the Augustinian monastery of Erfurt. We must not underestimate the choice of this specific monastic order and its implications.

First of all, the friary that Luther selected belonged to the Order of Hermits of Saint Augustine (*Ordo Eremitari Sancti Augustini*), a religious order highly devoted to its namesake and fully dedicated to the study of his works, two attitudes which Luther did not hesitate to embrace immediately. This tradition of Augustinian studies had already been flourishing for many decades before the birth of Luther.[9] One of the directives of the Rule of this order may help us to understand further the importance of Luther's life changing choice: "*The Lord grant* that you may observe all these precepts in a spirit of charity as lovers of spiritual beauty, giving forth the good odor of Christ in the holiness of your lives: *not as slaves living under the law but as men living in freedom under grace.*"[10] Indeed, his life, and especially the first years of his career, can be very concisely described borrowing the words of the earlier quote of Augustine: a continual desire that the Lord may grant[11] him to understand what it means not to be as a slave under the law but in freedom under grace,[12] and to live according to this knowledge.

The disputation took place on April 26, 1518. It was convened by Johann von Staupitz (1465–1524), the head of the Augustinian order in Germany and Luther's beloved Superior at the friary of Erfurt. Staupitz summoned the general chapter of the Augustinians to Heidelberg in order to give to his young disciple the opportunity to explain himself to the leadership of his own order. His colleagues and fellow canons welcomed

---

9. See Pani, *Lutero*, 17–19.

10. Augustine, *The Rule*, 8.1.

11. *Confessions* 10.31.45, 10.31.46. The famous prayer of Augustine, "Grant what thou commandest and then command what thou wilt," is present in many of his works, especially the ones of the Pelagian and Semi-Pelagian controversy.

12. In this regard, the passages of Augustine that may be mentioned are innumerable. It is enough to point to *The Spirit and the Letter* and *Against two Letters of the Pelagians*.

Luther to the city not as a dangerous heretic, but as a brilliant young theologian sincerely concerned for the spiritual condition of the church that he served faithfully as an appointed preacher and professor.[13] The outcome of the Disputation soon spread across Europe since Luther was already very famous among the church leadership because of his teaching, as he was very famous among the German population because of his 95 theses on the power and efficacy of indulgences.

> *Distrusting completely our own wisdom, according to that counsel of the Holy Spirit, »Do not rely on your own insight« (Prov. 3:5), we humbly present to the judgment of all those who wish to be here these theological paradoxes, so that it may become clear whether they have been deduced well or poorly from St. Paul, the especially chosen vessel and instrument of Christ, and also from St. Augustine, his most trustworthy interpreter.[14]*

The phrase, "St. Augustine, his most trustworthy interpreter," merits close attention. At this stage of his life, Luther considers Augustine the most faithful interpreter of Paul of Tarsus, the apostle whose letters have a position of pre-eminence in the study of the young Luther. It might be argued that this statement merely reflects an outward respect toward the main authority of Luther's order during a particular occasion where the leadership of the Augustinians was gathered. Nevertheless, there are other places where the young Luther clearly express his high estimation for the African theologian.

Luther once complained that, although Augustine was the greatest theologian after the apostles, his fellow canons were much more dedicated to the reading of Duns Scotus rather than to the African father.[15] It was the disputation *On the Power and Will of Man Apart from Grace* (*Questio de viribus et voluntate hominis sine gratia disputata*, September 25, 1516) that occasioned the definitive downfall of scholastic theology[16] at the

13 "I earnestly wish that nobody would imitate me in what I say here because my distress compels me and my office requires that I do so. For a teaching is understood best if one sees its relevance to the present condition of life. At the same time, I must perform my duty as a teacher who holds his office by apostolic authority. It is my duty to speak up whenever I see that something is done that is not right, even in higher places." Luther, *Romans*, 364.

14. Luther, *Heidelberg*, Second Preface.

15. "Hic est summus theologus, qui post apostolos scripserunt. Sed nos monachi non legimus eum, sed Scotum." Quoted in Pani, *Lutero*, 83.

16. What is relevant for our analysis is that, from Luther's point of view, scholastic theology as expounded by Duns Scotus, William of Ockham, and Gabriel Biel was characterized by Pelagianism, or, at least, Pelagianism was its logical conclusion. (See

university of Wittenberg. Scholasticism was replaced by Augustine and regular lessons on the Holy Scriptures, as Luther himself remarked the following year: "In our university, our theology and the theology of Saint Augustine, at the hands of God, reign and prosper. Aristotle is declining and at this point he will soon face a certain ruin. The *Sentences* are considered more and more a burden, and no one has any hope to gain auditors without this theology, that is, the Bible, or Augustine or another eminent doctor of the church."[17]

This emphatic preference for Augustine and biblical theology to the detriment of scholasticism was already evident in the commentary of Luther on the *Epistle of St. Paul to the Romans* (*Divi Pauli apostoli ad romanos Epistola*, 1515–1516), an extensive course of lectures on this apostolic epistle.[18] In this work, Augustine is quoted more than 150 times.[19] Moreover, in these lessons basically all the elements of Luther's peculiar theology of the cross are already present. This means that at this stage Luther already held his view of the righteousness of God (*Iustitia Dei*). Concerning Augustine's influence, the most quoted Augustinian work is *The Spirit and the Letter* (*De spiritu et Littera*, 412), present thirty-two times.[20] This short treatise of Augustine was fundamental for Luther's intellectual development since it gave him the authoritative confirmation necessary to his discovery, that is, that men are justified by grace alone through faith alone. To be more specific, Augustine helped Luther understand that the "righteousness" mentioned by Paul in his epistle to the Romans is not the attribute of God by which he is righteous, but it is the righteousness of Christ that God freely gives to man. We have Luther's own words in support of this. It is necessary to quote them extensively in order to have the entire context before us. This passage is also important for the understanding of the following chapters of this book.

---

the next chapter for a brief overview of Pelagian doctrine) We do not have time to give a developed account of the scholasticism that Luther opposed. For Luther and Scholasticism, see, for example, Atkinson, *Martin Luther and the Birth of Protestantism*, 34–54; McGrath, *Luther's Theology of the Cross*, 7–124; Wood, *Captive to the Word*, 31–40; Miegge, *Lutero*, 103–110.

17. "Theologia nostra et S. Augustinus prospere procedunt et regnant in nostra Universitate, Deo operante; Aristoteles descendit paulatim, inclinatus ad ruinam prope futuram perpetnam, mire fastidiuntur lectiones sententiariae. nec est, ut quis sibi audi tores sperare possit, nisi theologiam hanc, id est Bibliam aut S. Augustinum aliumve ecclesiasticae auctoritatis doctorem velit profiteri." Quoted in Pani, *Lutero*, 59–60.

18. This writing will often be taken into account throughout this book.

19. Pani, *Lutero*, 86.

20. *Ibid.*, 87.

For a long time I went astray [in the monastery] and didn't know what I was about. To be sure, I knew something, but I didn't know what it was until I came to the text in Rom 1 [:17], "He who through faith is righteous shall live." That text helped me. There I saw what righteousness Paul was talking about. Earlier in the text I read "righteousness." I related the abstract ["righteousness"] with the concrete ["the righteous One"] and became sure of my cause. I learned to distinguish between the righteousness of the law and the righteousness of the gospel. I lacked nothing before this except that I made no distinction between the law and the gospel. I regarded both as the same thing and held that there was no difference between Christ and Moses except the times in which they lived and their degrees of perfection. But when I discovered the proper distinction—namely, that the law is one thing and the gospel is another—I made myself free.

Meanwhile, I had already during that year returned to interpret the Psalter anew. I had confidence in the fact that I was more skillful, after I had lectured in the university on St. Paul's epistles to the Romans, to the Galatians, and the one to the Hebrews. I had indeed been captivated with an extraordinary ardor for understanding Paul in the Epistle to the Romans. But up till then it was not the cold blood about the heart, but a single word in Chapter 1[:17], "In it the righteousness of God is revealed," that had stood in my way. For I hated that word "righteousness of God," which, according to the use and custom of all the teachers, I had been taught to understand philosophically regarding the formal or active righteousness, as they called it, with which God is righteous and punishes the unrighteous sinner.

Though I lived as a monk without reproach, I felt that I was a sinner before God with an extremely disturbed conscience. I could not believe that he was placated by my satisfaction. I did not love, yes, I hated the righteous God who punishes sinners, and secretly, if not blasphemously, certainly murmuring greatly, I was angry with God, and said, "As if, indeed, it is not enough, that miserable sinners, eternally lost through original sin, are crushed by every kind of calamity by the law of the Decalogue, without having God add pain to pain by the gospel and also by the gospel threatening us with his righteousness and wrath!" Thus I raged with a fierce and troubled conscience. Nevertheless, I beat importunately upon Paul at that place, most ardently desiring to know what St. Paul wanted.

At last, by the mercy of God, meditating day and night, I gave heed to the context of the words, namely, "In it the righteousness of God is revealed, as it is written, 'He who through faith is righteous shall live.'" There I began to understand that the righteousness of God is that by which the righteous lives by a gift of God, namely by faith. And this is the meaning: the righteousness of God is revealed by the gospel, namely, the passive righteousness with which the merciful God justifies us by faith, as it is written, "He who through faith is righteous shall live." Here I felt that I was altogether born again and had entered paradise itself through open gates. There a totally other face of the entire Scripture showed itself to me. Thereupon I ran through the Scriptures from memory. I also found in other terms an analogy, as, the work of God, that is, what God does in us, the power of God, with which he makes us strong, the wisdom of God, with which he makes us wise, the strength of God, the salvation of God, the glory of God.[21]

The following part of this long quotation is the most important for our understanding of the importance of Augustine in Luther's intellectual development.

And I extolled my sweetest word with a love as great as the hatred with which I had before hated the word "righteousness of God." Thus that place in Paul was for me truly the gate to paradise. *Later I read Augustine's The Spirit and the Letter, where contrary to hope I found that he, too, interpreted God's righteousness in a similar way, as the righteousness with which God clothes us when he justifies us. Although this was heretofore said imperfectly and he did not explain all things concerning imputation clearly, it nevertheless was pleasing that God's righteousness with which we are justified was taught.* Armed more fully with these thoughts, I began a second time to interpret the Psalter. And the work would have grown into a large commentary, if I had not again been compelled to leave the work begun, because Emperor Charles V in the following year convened the diet at Worms.[22]

It is essential to notice how this quotation proves that Luther did not misunderstand, much less abuse, Augustine during his life study. On the contrary, Luther was well aware of Augustine's teaching. Regarding the matter of righteousness and justification, he knew perfectly that his view was not in all respects equal to Augustine's view. In particular, even though both Augustine and Luther agree that the righteousness in view is not the

---

21. Spitz and Lehman, *Luther's Works. Volume 34, Career of the Reformer IV,* 336–337.

22. *Ivi.* Emphasis added.

attribute of God but the righteousness that comes from God to men, he knew that Augustine often talked of the "infusion" of this righteousness in terms that he would never have used nor shared, preferring the purely legal term "imputation."[23] Nevertheless, this fact is not a point against Luther's teaching, but rather shows how Luther was fully conscious of the range of the developments that he was proposing, even though he did not anticipate the consequences and the historical developments that would follow.

All these historical and biographical factors make clear that the *Heidelberg Disputation* is an Augustinian disputation, and that it is intended to be so by its author.[24] The authorities whom Luther calls to his support reflect that same attitude of study that Luther had in his own life and the academic change with which he favored the university of Wittenberg. In fact, in addition to the highest authority of the apostle Paul,[25] Luther mentions also Paul's "most trustworthy interpreter," that is, Augustine. This is exactly the same change that Luther sought to bring to Wittenberg, namely, a relatively new course of study focused on the Scriptures (especially the apostle Paul) and on the worthiest of the church fathers (mainly Augustine, the greatest of them) instead of the *Sentences* of Peter Lombard and scholastic philosophy. The concise justification for an Augustinian reading of Luther presented here does not claim to be complete. Nevertheless, because of these elements, a deeper study of the Augustinian roots of Luther's philosophy of the cross is required.

It is necessary to clarify the methodology concerning the parallel that the research is seeking to establish between Augustine and Luther. Generally speaking, the vast majority of scholars who have been consulted with profit in the course of this study share the same hermeneutical approach to the subject here discussed. This approach tends to put much stress upon the differences between Luther and Augustine and, on the basis of these differences, there usually follows an evaluation of the influence that Augustine had on the doctrine of Luther. These evaluations most often obscure or deliberately avoid a positive treatment of the issue in light of the teachings shared by the authors. Certainly, it is important to

23. See Chapter 4.

24. "The aim of the Disputation and its proofs was to show that the theses were properly derived from these two authorities [Paul and Augustine]." Forde, *On Being a Theologian of the Cross*, 21.

25. Since Luther quotes passages not only from Paul but also from the Old and New Testament (the very first quoted Bible passage is from the Old Testament, i.e., Prov 3:5), "Paul" has to be intended in its secondary meaning as Holy Scripture in general.

have clear comparative studies of this kind, and even in this present work the points of disagreement between the two thinkers will not be utterly ignored. Nevertheless, it is true that this interpretative path can offer but an incomplete picture. First of all, in a comparative study there is no good reason to accord more importance to the dissimilarities than to the points of agreement. This approach is grounded in a conception of development of thought which is unrealistic and abstractly idealistic. In fact, it is to be fully expected that two theologians living more than one thousand years apart will have differences in their systems. For instance, it is clear that Augustine's doctrine of the imputation of justification is not in all respects equal to Luther's. However, from this fact the conclusion does not follow that Augustine was not a determining influence on Luther, especially if this assertion contradicts Luther's own words regarding Augustine which have been previously cited. Rather, I contend that a proper way to study the development of thought is to look in the past for the seeds which appear to be the theoretical causes of the development that will take place in the future. This book will adopt such a hermeneutical key and will try to substantiate it by looking at the positive incentives that Augustine has given to Luther in the development of his own thought. For this reason, the works of the two authors will be in sharp focus, and I will intervene with academic criticism toward them only when required. Augustine and Luther will be free to speak for themselves, and the present writer will let them explain with their own words rather that in his own words or in the words of another external spectator.

Before getting into our exploration of Augustine's presence in Martin Luther's thought, it will be helpful to set forth some theoretical premises. Luther says that we must engage in the reading of the theses "distrusting completely our own wisdom, according to that counsel of the Holy Spirit, 'Do not rely on your own insight' (Prov 3:5)" This can be very well described as the ethical and epistemological presupposition which grounds and opens the philosophy of the Theses. Every single philosopher in history bases his arguments on certain presuppositions. This assertion is not a criticism. In fact, to have presuppositions is necessary.

The same can be said regarding the concept of "authority." Luther is far removed from a world numbed by the dream of "freedom from the principle of authority." He is also far removed from an intellectual society haunted by the phantom of the unattainable ideal of "reason that critiques itself."[26] Every philosophical position appeals to one or more authorities,

---

26. Malatesta, "St. Augustine's Dialectic from the Modern Logic Standpoint. Logical

and on the basis of these authorities it proposes its conceptual path. This means that nobody who claims to be dedicated to the search of truth can claim to have a rational procedure utterly detached from all authority. Even here, this is not a criticism: to have one or more authorities for the development or establishment of a thought is necessary.

This also implies that it makes every possible difference if we presuppose, for instance, a Pelagian anthropology rather than an Augustinian anthropology, a difference that necessarily results in two radically different epistemologies. These considerations are important to bear in mind because, in the thought of Luther (as well as in that of Augustine), ethics and epistemology are mutually related. However, ethics has a sort of pre-eminence over epistemology. In fact, our epistemology is dictated by our ethical premises. This means that according to our ethics we will formulate a specific epistemology. By "ethics" and "ethical premises" we mean not only our convictions in the field of morals, but also a position regarding the moral structure of man himself. The ethical structure of our soul defines not only what we know and how we know it, but also what we *want* to know; not only what we do and how we do it, but also what we *want* to do. Every schism between "theoretical reason" and "ethical reason" is therefore completely ruled out.[27] Our reason and our consequent epistemology are not at all independent of our inner ethical condition.[28]

Now, the presuppositions from which Luther starts are Christian presuppositions. Being Christian premises, "they have been deduced well . . . from Paul, and also from his most trustworthy interpreter, St. Augustine."[29]

Analysis of *Contra Academicos* 3.10.22–13.29," 115–116.

27. Malatesta, "La problematica linguistica nel *Contra Academicos* alla luce della filosofia del linguaggio contemporanea," 59–63.

28. "Being comes before doing, but being acted upon comes before being [Prius est enim esse quam operari, prius auem pati quam esse]. Hence becoming, being, acting, follow one another." Luther, *Romans*, 321. "The schoolmen grant and teach, that in order of nature, being goeth before working; for naturally the tree is before the fruit. Again, in philosophy they grant, that a work morally wrought is not good, except there be first a right judgment of reason, and a good will or intent; so then they will have a right judgment of reason, and a good intent to go before the work; that is, they make the person morally righteous before the work. Contrariwise, in divinity, and in spiritual matters, where they ought most of all to do so, such dull and senseless asses they are, that they pervert and turn all quite contrary, placing the work before right judgment of reason and goo intent." Luther, *Commentary on Galatians*, 152. These reflections about the circular relationship between epistemology and ethics are from Marco Barone, "Agostino e l'Accademia Scettica nel *Contra Academicos*." BA Thesis, Università degli Studi di Napoli "Federico II," 2012, 58–62.

29. Luther, *Heidelberg*, Second Preface.

This means that the authoritative foundation of his presupposition is, first of all, Scripture and, secondly and as a complement to Scripture, Augustine of Hippo. Hence the question: why must we distrust our own wisdom, and do so completely? One should do that because, from Luther's Biblical point of view, man has fallen from a state of innocence into a state of misery, depravity, and death. Because of this fall, man has become spiritually (i.e., ethically) blind, and he has now lost his free will, which is free only to do evil (Theses 13–16). His will is now enslaved to sin, and he is neither able nor willing to do good works (Theses 1–12). Man always looks for moral principles that fit his own fallenness, but for Luther the truth is that true morality is revealed by God in his law, which must be kept perfectly and with perfect love. However, man is not only unable to do this, but is also inclined to the exact opposite (Theses 16–18, 1–12). To make matters even worse, man looks for the solution to this ethical corruption in himself, undergoing a never ending circle of fallenness, instead of looking outside of himself to the divinely revealed way (Theses 19–24).[30]

Considering the ethical nature of man, what kind of "wisdom" can he claim to have? He will claim the possession of apparent wisdom, which is actually foolishness. However, what he really needs is apparent foolishness, which is actually wisdom. He needs a philosophy of the cross. But we are now entering the Disputation itself, and this unclear Lutheran terminology will be explained in light of its Augustinian origin. We can now focus on the Theses more specifically and clarify many terms and concepts that this introduction has only mentioned. We will start by looking at the Augustinianism of Luther's *Heidelberg Disputation*.

---

30. I follow the thematic division of Forde, *On Being a Theologian of the Cross*, 21–22. In his division, Forde maintains the order that Luther has given to his paradoxes. As has already been pointed out, the order has been changed in order to facilitate the fluency of the analysis.

CHAPTER 2

FREE WILL

THE ISSUE OF FREE will is the first topic that this book will discuss. The theoretical reason in support of this choice has already been given, and will become gradually clearer. In order to understand the content of Luther's and Augustine's philosophy and the reason why they held such ideas, it is essential to grasp first their anthropology, that is, their doctrine of the moral constitution of human nature. *What* is man in his relation to God, to other men, and to himself? Once we establish this point, the rest of their positions will be easier to expound. In all of this, even though we have said that ethics has a sort of priority over epistemology, this priority is merely chronological and not qualitative. This means that for man, to be enlightened, ethics and epistemology are equally important. However, the knowledge of ethics (i.e., the ethical constitution of his own nature) is what comes first in order properly to understand the supreme epistemological principle (as we will see, true ethics *comes from* this epistemological principle, that is, the incarnation of the Logos, the cross of Christ). Therefore, it must be borne in mind that the relationship between ethics and epistemology is not hierarchical, but it is in a sense cyclical: without the right epistemology we cannot understand ethics, and without the right ethics every epistemological attempt is erroneous.[1]

---

1. I will use the terms "philosophy" and "theology" interchangeably. My conviction is that every theology is necessarily also a philosophy in the broadest sense. It is true that every philosophy is not necessarily a theology, but it is true that every philosophy necessarily intends a theology in the broadest sense, that is, as an intellectual and

Augustine and Luther were participants in two of the fiercest battles ever engaged on this subject: the controversy with the Pelagians[2] and Semi-Pelagians[3] and the dispute with Erasmus of Rotterdam, respectively. Moreover, the latter debate occasioned the writing of Luther's *magnum opus*, *The Bondage of the Will*, while the former triggered the production of the most important works of Augustine in which we find his theology at its highest development and systematization, namely, his anti-Pelagian

---

practical attitude toward God or the idea of God. Moreover, independently from the conviction of the present writer, Augustine and Luther lived in ages where the distinction between philosophy and theology was not as sharp as in the modern one. This is true especially for Augustine. In fact, his philosophy is his theology, and vice-versa.

2. Augustine himself offers a summary of the teaching of Pelagius: "Then follow sundry statements charged against Pelagius, which are said to be found among the opinions of his disciple Caelestius: how that '*Adam was created mortal, and would have died whether he had sinned or not sinned; that Adam's sin injured only himself and not the human race; that the law no less than the gospel leads us to the kingdom; that there were sinless men previous to the coming of Christ; that new-born infants are in the same condition as Adam was before the fall; that the whole human race does not, on the one hand, die through Adam's death or transgression, nor, on the other hand, does the whole human race rise again through the resurrection of Christ.*'" Augustine, *On the Proceedings of Pelagius*, 11.23. This summary is brief, but it is sufficient for our goal. See also Augustine, *Against Two Letters of the Pelagians*, 3.8.24–9.25; *On Heresies*, 88.1–7; Warfield, "Augustine and the Pelagian Controversy," especially 297–298;

3. This is how Schaff sums up the Semi-Pelagian teaching: "Semi-Pelagianism is a somewhat vague and indefinite attempt at reconciliation, hovering midway between the sharply marked systems of Pelagius and Augustine, taking off the edge of each, and inclining now to the one, now to the other. The name was introduced during the scholastic age, but the system of doctrine, in all essential points, was formed in Southern France in the fifth century, during the latter years of Augustine's life and soon after his death. It proceeded from the combined influence of the pre-Augustinian synergism and monastic legalism. Its leading idea is, that divine grace and the human will jointly accomplish the work of conversion and sanctification, and that ordinarily man must take the first step. It rejects the Pelagian doctrine of the moral soundness of man, but rejects also the Augustinian doctrine of the entire corruption and bondage of the natural man, and substitutes the idea of a diseased or crippled state of the voluntary power. It disowns the Pelagian conception of grace as a mere external auxiliary; but also, quite as decidedly, the Augustinian doctrines of the sovereignty, irresistibleness, and limitation of grace; and affirms the necessity and the internal operation of grace with and through human agency, a general atonement through Christ, and a predestination to salvation conditioned by the foreknowledge of faith. The union of the Pelagian and Augustinian elements thus attempted is not, however, an inward organic coalescence, but rather a mechanical and arbitrary combination, which really satisfies neither the one interest nor the other, but commonly leans to the Pelagian side." Schaff, *History of the Christian Church Vol. 3*, 857–858. See also Warfield, "Augustine and the Pelagian Controversy," 305–306. For primary sources, see Augustine, *Letters*, 217; 226; 226. What is of interest for our analysis is that, in Semi-Pelagianism and also in Pelagianism, salvation *ultimately depends* not on God's work, but on man's activity.

and anti-Semipelagian works.[4] This is not the place to discuss the history of these two events. It is sufficient to say that these two debates have many elements in common. In fact, not only are many of Erasmus' arguments and objections to Luther very similar, if not identical, to those proposed by Augustine's adversaries, but Luther will adopt and develop many of the arguments which Augustine used during that dispute.[5]

As was noted in the introduction, Luther quotes Augustine extensively in his early works. Augustine's name is mentioned eleven times, and six of the theological theses of the *Heidelberg Disputation* mention Augustine, with a total of four direct quotations. Considering the brevity of the document, these statistics are quite noteworthy. Yet, what is most important is the intellectual presence of Augustine in the document, and not merely his nominal presence. For the sake of clarity and brevity, we will explain the Theses of Luther only when necessary. Several works have already very well met this need.[6] We will now focus our attention upon the Augustinianism of the *Heidelberg Disputation*. We remember that the following analysis will provide us with a launching pad from which to offer a further evaluation of the philosophical relevance of Luther's philosophy of the cross.

It stands to reason that the nature of this research compels us to a technical discussion of theology. The reader is asked to exercise patience through the more theological sections of the book which will discuss the more philosophical conclusions in its final section. After all, it is true that the history of philosophy cannot be properly and deeply understood without the history of theology, and vice-versa.

> *13. Free will, after the fall, exists in name only, and as long as it does what it is able to do, it commits a mortal sin.*[7]

4. By this I only mean to say that the works written on the occasion of the Pelagian and anti-Pelagian controversy are the most developed and clearest works that we can read in order to learn about the core of Augustinianism, that is, Augustine's theology of absolute grace.

5. See Luther's usage of Augustine's works in some of his most famous works, such as *The Bondage of the Will* and *Lectures on Romans*.

6. See, for example, von Loewenich, *Luther's Theology of the Cross*; Miegge, *Lutero*, 143–171; Forde, *On Being a Theologian of the Cross*; McGrath, *Luther's Theology of the Cross: Martin Luther's Theological Breakthrough*.

7. "The first part is clear, for the will is captive and subject to sin. Not that it is nothing, but that it is not free except to do evil. According to John 8:34, 36, 'Every one who commits sin is a slave to sin.' 'So if the Son makes you free, you will be free indeed.' Hence St. Augustine says in his book *The Spirit and the Letter*: 'Free will without grace has the power to do nothing but sin;' and in the second book of *Against Julian*, 'You

We should start with a definition of "free will." We may adopt a definition that is taken from a later work of Luther, *The Bondage of the Will*. "I conceive of 'free-will' in this context as a power of the human will by which a man may apply himself to those things that lead to eternal salvation, or turn away from the same."[8] This definition is not Luther's, but is a definition given by Erasmus of Rotterdam. However, this fact does not make the definition irrelevant to our analysis. On the contrary, since *Heidelberg Disputation* 13–18 aims to disprove a certain doctrine of free will (properly summarized by the words of Erasmus), the definition in question will help us to understand what Luther wants to tell us through Augustine.

By "fall" Luther means the fall of Adam and Eve as reported in the Biblical book of Genesis, chapter 3. It is helpful to resume briefly what Augustine taught on this topic. Augustine, like Luther, considers man as a creature, created out of the dust in the image and likeness of the Triune God and originally placed at the head of creation. He was created holy and righteous, with a good will and able to keep the moral law of God perfectly and, more importantly, to enjoy the presence of God in friendship. Under the instigation of the devil, the first man willingly and consciously sinned against God's command.[9] Adam was mankind's federal head and each and every man was represented by him.[10] This means that the consequences of Adam's fall extend to all those whom he represented.[11] It is important to note that Augustine, in opposition to the Pelagians, believes that among these consequences is much more than a mere bad example delivered to humanity.[12] As a consequence, spiritual and physical death and corruption came upon him and upon all human beings derived from him.[13] All men, newborn babies included, are therefore spiritually dead.[14] Man is ethically deceased, for he is spiritually "dead both in soul and body: in soul, because

---

call the will free, but in fact it is an enslaved will,' and in many other places. The second part is clear from what has been said above and from the verse in Hos 13:9, 'Israel, you are bringing misfortune upon yourself, for your salvation is alone with me,' and from similar passages." Proof 13.

8. Luther, *The Bondage of the Will*, 137.

9. Augustine, *On Rebuke and grace*, 28; *The City of God*, 14.11; *On Man's Perfection in Righteousness*, 2.13.

10. Augustine, *The City of God*, 12:28.

11. *Ibid.*, 13:14.

12. Augustine, *On Merit and the Forgiveness of Sins, and the Baptism of Infants*, 1:10; *On Nature and Grace*, 21.

13. Augustine, *Enchiridion*, 25–27.

14. Augustine, *On Marriage and Concupiscence*, 1.47; *The Gospel of John*, 44.1

of sin; in body, because of the punishment of sin, and through this also in body because of sin."[15] This is the theological anthropology that constitutes the context we must bear in mind as we proceed.

In this regard, we have to remember that Augustine does not share our society's modern individualistic thinking. For Augustine, the world is not composed of individuals basically separated from each other. He rather considered the members of families, tribes, peoples, and nations as mutually and organically related to each other. Most importantly, Augustine takes this concept of corporate responsibility from Scripture, the main source of his thought.[16] For Augustinianism, Adam was the federal head of all humanity, where by humanity is intended an organic whole and not a collection of individuals. In Adam, all mankind was represented. This implies that, when Adam fell, all humanity fell. Thus, Adam transmitted to his posterity not only the consequences of his sin, but also the guilt.

Now, even though Augustine sometimes uses different terminology and gives emphasis to aspects that Luther seems to neglect, the nature of the human will is a subject where Luther and Augustine appear to show the greatest agreement. In accordance with thesis 13, Augustine believed that after the fall of man into sin from his original state of righteousness and holiness, the term "free will" is nothing but a term. This will, from God's point of view, is able only to sin. As the proof attached to the theses explains, this does not mean that man has no will whatsoever: "Not that it is nothing, but that it is not free except to do evil."[17] Man has a will, but it is 'captive and subjected to sin' and, by definition, something or someone that is captive is not free. Luther quotes Augustine twice in support of the first part of the proof of the thesis. The first quote is from *The Spirit and the Letter* where Augustine explicitly argues that "man's free-will, indeed, avails for nothing except to sin, if he knows not the way of truth."[18] Of course, he is referring to man's free will as fallen and not as created. The second quote offered by Luther is from *Against Julian* 2.8.23. If it is true that man's will is enslaved to sin, Luther concludes that the second part of the thesis follows. In fact, man's will "as long as it does what it is able to do, it commits a mortal sin," because the will is able to do only what is in accordance with its nature. Because his ethical nature is sinful, man's

15. Augustine, *On the Trinity*, 4.3.5.

16. See, for example, Rom 5:12: "Wherefore, as by one man sin entered into the world, and death by sin; and so death passed upon all men, for that all have sinned."

17. Luther, *Heidelberg*, Proof 13.

18. Augustine, *The Spirit and the Letter*, 3.5.

resulting deeds cannot be anything but sinful. The African theologian was always prone to avoid terminological disputes and this is the reason why he uses and accepts the term. Nevertheless, free will is "only a term" for Luther as for Augustine. While rebuking Julian and those who believe that a perfect moral life is possible in this earthly life, Augustine shows a clear hint of his unhappiness with this term. He believes that the adjective that modifies "will" should not be "free" but rather "slave,"[19] that is, enslaved to sin.

Thesis 13 also speaks of man's necessity to sin. The term 'necessity' must not be understood as "compulsion." Although both Augustine and Luther hold strong views on predestination, they never assert that man is dragged to sin against his own will. On the contrary, man not only *wants* to sin, but he *delights* in such sinful activity, just as Adam and Eve delighted in their willful disobedience to God. By "necessity" Augustine and Luther mean that mankind, apart from regenerating grace, can do nothing but sin because the nature of the source of his action is sinful, and here "necessity" is explained.[20] And this corrupt state must not be attributed to God who created man free, but to the first man who misused the freedom God gave him, so plunging himself and his descendants into sinfulness and unrighteousness, destroying that freedom.[21]

> *14. Free will, after the fall, has power to do good only in a passive capacity, but it can always do evil in an active capacity.*[22]

Thesis 14 is strictly connected to the preceding. Augustine is clearly present, although no specific passage from any of his works is mentioned. In fact, Luther says in the proof that "St. Augustine . . . proves this same thesis

19. ". . . non libero, vel potius servo propriae voluntatis arbitrio." Augustine, *Against Julian*, 2.8.23

20. "It came by the freedom of choice that man was with sin; but a penal corruption closely followed thereon, and out of the liberty produced necessity . . . With these necessities upon us, we are either unable to understand what we want, or else (while having the wish) we are not strong enough to accomplish what we have come to understand." Augustine, *On Man's Perfection in Righteousness*, 4.9. "After he [Adam] voluntarily sinned, we who have descended from his stock were plunged into necessity." Augustine, *Acts or Disputation Against Fortunatus the Manichaean*, 22.

21. Augustine, *Enchiridion*, 30.

22. "An illustration will make the meaning of this thesis clear. Just as a dead man can do something toward life only in his original capacity (*in vitam solum subiective*), so can he do something toward death in an active manner while he lives. Free will, however, is dead, as demonstrated by the dead whom the Lord has raised up, as the holy teachers of the church say. St. Augustine, moreover, proves this same thesis in his various writings against the Pelagians." Luther, *Heidelberg*, Proof 14.

in his various writings against the Pelagians."[23] We can indeed find several places in those that will explain and support what Luther is saying. As we have seen, Augustine uses the term 'free-will' only to avoid debates about terminology . Nevertheless, Augustine believes that "free will itself is ascribable to God's grace, in other words, to the gifts of God—not only as to its existence, but also as to its being good, that is, to its conversion to doing the commandments of God."[24] Only an omnipotent deliverer can set free the enslaved will of man. Only God is able to work in the heart of man in such a way that man becomes willing and able to turn to the Highest Good, activities that he is totally incapable and unwilling to accomplish by himself.[25] "[The Pelagians] place so much in free will by which man is plunged into the abyss, as to say that by making good use of it man deserves grace—although no man can make good use of it except by grace, which is not repaid according to debt, but is given freely by God's mercy."[26]

This concept is very similar to what Luther means by "passivity," or "passive capacity." Augustine does not mean that man is a puppet mechanically moved by God. In fact, it has been previously mentioned that the will is not nothing at all: man certainly has a will and he certainly wills. What Augustine means is that this will is spiritually fallen and dead *with reference to God* and *with reference to what is good according to God* (who is the highest Good, good in himself), and not according to man's judgment or opinion. The will is restored to freedom by the mere activity of God's grace, which is given to certain people independently of their inner or outer activity and volition. Therefore, we see that, on the one hand, Augustine does not deny the existence of a will, which he reluctantly calls free will. On the other hand, Augustine claims that man is in a state of spiritual fallenness, a fall that has made man's will corrupt and able only to do evil in the sight of God, even when his actions appear good and charitable from an outward or human point of view. Because of this fall, man's restoration to real freedom is, from the beginning, an act of God

23. *Ivi.*

24. Augustine, *On Merit and the Forgiveness of Sins, and the Baptism of Infants,* 2.6.7.

25. "He is drawn to Christ to whom it is given to believe in Christ. Therefore the power is given that they who believe in Him should become the sons of God, since this very thing is given, that they believe in Him. And unless this power be given from God, out of free will there can be none; because it will not be free for good if the deliverer have not made it free; but in evil he has a free will in whom a deceiver, either secret or manifest, has grafted the love of wickedness, or he himself has persuaded himself of it." Augustine, *Against Two Letters of the Pelagians,* 1.3.6.

26. *Ibid.,* 1.24.42.

where man's will is involved only as the object and not as the subject of this supernatural regeneration.[27]

> *15. Nor could free will remain in a state of innocence, much less do good, in an active capacity, but only in its passive capacity (subiectiva potentia).*[28]

After discussing the state of mankind considered in its fallen state, in thesis 15 Luther makes the same point also in relation to mankind in the state of innocence, represented by Adam, before the fall. Luther disagrees with the medieval theologian Peter Lombard who says that before the fall man was able to "prevail" thanks to the active capacity of his free will.[29] According to the grace of creation, man was able by himself to persevere and to remain in the state of innocence, if he wanted to. Otherwise, according to Lombard, it would be impossible to attribute any fault to man for his own fall. Luther, on the contrary, believes that Adam was totally dependent on God's gracious sustainment also before the fall, when he had a free and righteous will. He could not remain in that state of righteousness merely by a natural inner capacity independent of God's action (*potentia activa*). Instead, he depended upon God's active and gracious work in him (*potentia subiectiva*). Augustine says something very similar in the work quoted by Luther in the proof of the thesis. It is an argument that requires more precise explanation.

Even though Lombard quotes Augustine with approval, Luther says that the scholastic theologian actually misunderstands him. *On Rebuke and Grace* 11. 31–33 clearly declares that the first man could do good and persevere not by mere virtue of his own creaturely gifts, but by a supernatural gracious gift continually sustaining him . The fact that the holy and righteous Adam fell is clear evidence that "free will is sufficient for evil, but

---

27. Se also *Ibid.*, 2.5.9.; 2.10.23; 3.8.24; 3.9.25.

28. "The Master of the Sentences (Peter Lombard), quoting Augustine, states, 'By these testimonies it is obviously demonstrated that man received a righteous nature and a good will when he was created, and also the help by means of which he could prevail. Otherwise it would appear as though he had not fallen because of his own fault.» He speaks of the active capacity (*potentia activa*), which is obviously contrary to Augustine's opinion in his book *Concerning Reprimand and Grace* (*De Correptione et Gratia*), where the latter puts it in this way: «He received the ability to act, if he so willed, but he did not have the will by means of which he could act.» By «ability to act» he understands the original capacity (*potentia subiectiva*), and by «will by means of which he could,» the active capacity (*potentia activa*). The second part (of the thesis), however, is sufficiently clear from the same reference to the Master." Luther, *Heidelberg*, Proof 15.

29. Lombard, *Libri Quatuor Sententiarum*, 2.24.1.

is too little for good, unless it is aided by Omnipotent Good."[30] Augustine applies this last sentence not to man as fallen, but to man as considered *before* the fall in his state of innocence. In the following paragraph, which is the section quoted by Luther in the proof for thesis 15, Augustine repeats that Adam "needed the aid of grace to continue in it [in the state on innocence], and without this aid he could not do this at all,"[31] and this was because "he had received the ability if he would, but he had not the will for what he could; for if he had possessed it, he would have persevered."[32] Augustine continues comparing and differentiating between the freedom of Adam and the freedom that God creates in the hearts of men and that will be made perfect in the life to come: "to be able not to sin, and not to be able to sin; to be able not to die, and not to be able to die; to be able not to forsake good, and not to be able to forsake good. For the first man was able not to sin, was able not to die, was able not to forsake good . . . Therefore the first liberty of the will was to be able not to sin, the last will be much greater, not to be able to sin; the first immortality was to be able not to die, the last will be much greater, not to be able to die; the first was the power of perseverance, to be able not to forsake good—the last will be the felicity of perseverance, not to be able to forsake good."[33]

---

30. "The first man had not that grace by which he should never will to be evil; but assuredly he had that in which if he willed to abide he would never be evil, and without which, moreover, he could not by free will be good, but which, nevertheless, by free will he could forsake. God, therefore, did not will even him to be without His grace, which He left in his free will; because free will is sufficient for evil, but is too little for good, unless it is aided by Omnipotent Good. And if that man had not forsaken that assistance of his free will, he would always have been good; but he forsook it, and he was forsaken. Because such was the nature of the aid, that he could forsake it when he would, and that he could continue in it if he would; but not such that it could be brought about that he would. This first is the grace which was given to the first Adam; but more powerful than this is that in the second Adam. For the first is that whereby it is effected that a man may have righteousness if he will; the second, therefore, can do more than this, since by it it is even effected that he will, and will so much, and love with such ardour, that by the will of the Spirit he overcomes the will of the flesh, that lusts in opposition to it. Nor was that, indeed, a small grace by which was demonstrated even the power of free will, because man was so assisted that without this assistance he could not continue in good, but could forsake this assistance if he would. But this latter grace is by so much the greater, that it is too little for a man by its means to regain his lost freedom; it is too little, finally, not to be able without it either to apprehend the good or to continue in good if he will, unless he is also made to will." Augustine, *On Corruption and Grace*, 11.31.

31. *Ibid.*, 11.32.

32. *Ivi.*

33. *Ibid.*, 12.33.

It seems sufficiently clear that Luther is echoing the language of Augustine. If original free will, according to its own nature, was unable to persevere in good when left to itself, how is it possible to claim that man's current fallen will may be free to make a neutral choice between good and evil, or even to expect it to be able do what God defines good? The following thesis defines this kind of ethical presumption.

> 16. *The person who believes that he can obtain grace by doing what is in him adds sin to sin so that he becomes doubly guilty.*[34]

For Luther, these claims are rather presumptuous and are in themselves evidence of the corruption of man's will and its spiritual death. This is a moral presupposition which, in the eyes of God, only adds sin to the already sinful condition of man and to his preexisting original sin. In fact, we need to remember that for Luther sin is not merely wrong practice or the individual sin of commission and omission. Sin, according to Luther, is the ethical corruption of the entire being of man. It is not a matter of works, but of nature. Since the nature of man is corrupt, the fruits of this nature will also necessarily be so.

The first part of the proof appears to be clearly Augustinian. Here Luther refers to those who believe that the grace of God can be obtained by a mere external obedience to the precepts of God's law. This belief presupposes two positions. The first is that man in this way would be entitled to "merit" something from God, that is, a holy Creator would owe something to a sinful creature for his works, which are defiled by sin. Secondly,

---

34. "On the basis of what has been said, the following is clear: While a person is doing what is in him, he sins and seeks himself in everything. But if he should suppose that through sin he would become worthy of or prepared for grace, he would add haughty arrogance to his sin and not believe that sin is sin and evil is evil, which is an exceedingly great sin. As Jer 2:13 says, 'For my people have committed two evils: they have forsaken me, the fountain of living waters, and hewed out cisterns for themselves, broken cisterns, that can hold no water,' that is, through sin they are far from me and yet they presume to do good by their own ability. Now you ask: What then shall we do? Shall we go our way with indifference because we can do nothing but sin? I would reply: By no means. But, having heard this, fall down and pray for grace and place your hope in Christ in whom is our salvation, life, and resurrection. For this reason we are so instructed—for this reason the law makes us aware of sin so that, having recognized our sin, we may seek and receive grace. Thus God 'gives grace to the humble' (1 Pet 5:5), and 'whoever humbles himself will be exalted' (Matt 23:12). The law humbles, grace exalts. The law effects fear and wrath, grace effects hope and mercy. Through the law comes knowledge of sin (Rom 3:20), through knowledge of sin, however, comes humility, and through humility grace is acquired. Thus an action which is alien to God's nature (*opus alienum dei*) results in a deed belonging to his very nature (*opus proprium*): he makes a person a sinner so that he may make him righteous." Luther, *Heidelberg*, Proof 16.

the teaching that man could by himself operate a sort of self-resurrection would be a denial of what God has revealed to be the ethical condition of man, i.e., his sinfulness and corruption. Augustine, on the contrary, with Luther, holds that only God "by his grace removes from the non-believers their heart of stone and that he anticipates in human beings the merits of their good wills so that he may prepare their wills by his antecedent grace, not so that grace might be given because of their antecedent merits of their wills."[35] For the Augustinian message of Luther, there is no place for any kind of theological humanism or for any concept of "merit," religious or not.

The second part of proof 16, in connection with theses 17 and 18, may appear at first reading to move unexpectedly into a discussion about the law and righteousness. A closer consideration, however, suggests otherwise. In fact, according to Luther it is not enough to know that our will and nature are ethically fallen and corrupt, unable to will and do good. What we also need to know is *who* or *what* establishes what is this *good* that man is unable to achieve. *What* exactly is man unable and unwilling to do? The answer is simple: the moral law of God, basically, the ten commandments. It is the knowledge of this law that makes us aware of what we are.

> *17. Nor does speaking in this manner give cause for despair, but for arousing the desire to humble oneself and seek the grace of Christ.*[36]

> *18. It is certain that man must utterly despair of his own ability before he is prepared to receive the grace of Christ.*[37]

35. Augustine, *Letters*, 217.7.28.

36. "This is clear from what has been said, for, according to the gospel, the kingdom of heaven is given to children and the humble (Mark 10:14,16), and Christ loves them. They cannot be humble who do not recognize that they are damnable whose sin smells to high heaven. Sin is recognized only through the law. It is apparent that not despair, but rather hope, is preached when we are told that we are sinners. Such preaching concerning sin is a preparation for grace, or it is rather the recognition of sin and faith in such preaching. Yearning for grace wells up when recognition of sin has arisen. A sick person seeks the physician when he recognizes the seriousness of his illness. Therefore one does not give cause for despair or death by telling a sick person about the danger of his illness, but, in effect, one urges him to seek a medical cure. To say that we are nothing and constantly sin when we do the best we can does not mean that we cause people to despair (unless we are fools); rather, we make them concerned about the grace of our Lord Jesus Christ." Luther, *Heidelberg*, Proof 17.

37. "The law wills that man despair of his own ability, for it »leads him into hell« and »makes him a poor man« and shows him that he is a sinner in all his works, as the Apostle does in Rom. 2 and 3:9, where he says, »I have already charged that all men

Even though this point will be examined further and with more preci-
sion, especially in chapters 3 and 4, it will be worthwhile to introduce a
few concepts here. The ethical constitution of man is made known by the
knowledge of the moral law of God contained in the Scripture. God demands that this law be observed fully and perfectly. Luther and Augustine
base their theistic moral philosophy on the authority of Scripture. We
must notice the "opposition" that Luther is making here. Thesis 17 says
that "speaking in this manner" does not "give cause for despair," while
thesis 18 says that "man must utterly despair." Luther loved to express
himself by setting forth apparent paradoxes in order to make his point.
However, the contradiction is only apparent. In fact, Luther does not mean
that man must lose every hope, but that man must despair "of his own
ability." Despairing of his own ability, man is ready to receive that Wisdom
who comes to him from the outside and who is able graciously to restore
in him true freedom, namely, Jesus Christ.

Augustine's approach is very similar to Luther's. Augustine always
fought against "these proud and haughty people' who 'do not maintain free
will by purifying it, but demolish it by exaggerating it."[38] Augustine cannot
allow any moralistic philosophy nor any legalistic theology to poison the
teaching of grace which is at the center of his intellectual and personal
life. "What object, then, can this man gain by accounting the law and the
teaching to be the grace whereby we are helped to work righteousness?
For, in order that it may help much, it must help us to feel our need of
grace. No man, indeed, is able to fulfill the law through the law. 'Love is the
fulfilling of the law' (Rom 13:10). And the love of God is not shed abroad in
our hearts by the law, but by the Holy Ghost, which is given unto us (Rom
5:5). Grace, therefore, is pointed at by the law, in order that the law may
be fulfilled by grace."[39] While every other philosophy views the law as an
end in itself and understands man as inherently able to fulfill it (not only
the Divine law, but any kind of law), Augustine believes that the law is the
pedagogue (or schoolmaster) that instructs us about our utter hopeless-
ness, pointing and directing us to the justice that comes from outside and
that we can find in the work of the incarnate Word in Jesus Christ.[40]

---

are under the power of sin.« However, he who acts simply in accordance with his ability and believes that he is thereby doing something good does not seem worthless to
himself, nor does he despair of his own strength. Indeed, he is so presumptuous that he
strives for grace in reliance on his own strength." *Ibid.*, Proof 18.

38. Augustine, *Against Two Letters of the Pelagians*, 1.4.8.

39. Augustine, *On the Grace of Christ and on Original Sin*, 1.10.

40. "The law, therefore, by teaching and commanding what cannot be fulfilled

The proofs of theses 17 and 18 contain several typically Augustinian expressions. We have seen that in *Letters* 145.3 Augustine condemns
those who trust in their own strength, who believe that they are able to
fulfill the law and to establish their own moralistic and philosophical righteousness in opposition to that divine righteousness which is freely given
and received. Moreover, in proof 17 we can find the parallel of God as a
"physician," the "one" who "urges him to seek a medical cure." Augustine
uses this figure in several places to depict the work of God through the
law which is externally unpleasant and painful (in fact, the law kills and
humbles), but which actually is performed for the good of the "patient" in
bringing him to grace (in fact, grace exalts and sets free).[41]

---

without grace, demonstrates to man his weakness, in order that the weakness thus
proved may resort to the Saviour, by whose healing the will may be able to do what in
its feebleness it found impossible. So, then, the law brings us to faith, faith obtains the
Spirit in fuller measure, the Spirit sheds love abroad in us, and love fulfils the law. For
this reason the law is called a 'schoolmaster' (Gal 3:23), under whose threatenings and
severity 'whosoever shall call upon the name of the Lord shall be delivered' (Joel 2:32).
But 'how shall they call on Him in whom they have not believed?' (Rom 10:14) Wherefore unto them that believe and call on Him the quickening Spirit is given (2 Cor 3:6),
lest the letter without the Spirit should kill them. But by the Holy Ghost, which is given
unto us, the love of God is shed abroad in our hearts? (Rom 5:5) So that the words of
the same apostle, 'Love is the fulfilling of the law" (Rom 13:10), are realized. So the law
is good to the man who uses it lawfully (1 Tim 1:8); and he uses it lawfully who, understanding wherefore it was given, betakes himself, under the pressure of its threatenings,
to grace, which sets him free. Whoever unthankfully despises this grace, by which the
ungodly are justified, and trusts in his own strength, as if he thereby could fulfil the law,
being ignorant of God's righteousness, and going about to establish his own righteousness, is not submitting himself to the righteousness of God (Rom 10:3); and thus the
law becomes to him not a help to pardon, but the bond fastening his guilt to him. Not
that the law is evil, but because sin works death in such persons by that which is good
(Rom 7:13). For by occasion of the commandment he sins more grievously who, by
the commandment, knows how evil are the sins which he commits." Augustine, *Letters*, 145.3. I have added the Biblical references to show the adherence of Augustine to
Pauline teaching. Paul is quoted or implicitly mentioned at least eight times.

41. "For there was need to prove to man how corruptly weak he was, so that against
his iniquity, the holy law brought him no help towards good, but rather increased than
diminished his iniquity; seeing that the law entered, that the offense might abound; that
being thus convicted and confounded, he might see not only that he needed a physician, but also God as his helper so to direct his steps that sin should not rule over him,
and he might be healed by betaking himself to the help of the divine mercy; and in this
way, where sin abounded grace might much more abound—not through the merit of
the sinner, but by the intervention of his Helper." Augustine, *The Spirit and the Letter*,
6.9. See also *On Nature and Grace*, 27.31; *On Christian Doctrine*, 1.14.13; *First Epistle of
John*, 10.1. This concept appears also in the early works of Augustine, see, for instance,
On True Religion 34, *Expositions on the Psalms*, 21.2.4

Augustine's account of his own personal and intellectual pilgrimage shows the same full distrust and continual battle with his own will. For example, in the very first chapter of his *Confessions*, Augustine asks God and himself how man "who bears about with him his mortality, the witness of his sin"[42] is supposed to praise and know him. In fact, he goes on to say that human existence itself should be more properly named "living death." and not "deadly life." This is because, even though man is alive in his body, his will with his soul is spiritually dead. Considering the importance that Augustine ascribed to the inner life, to his soul and will, and given that the will of man, apart from divine grace, is enslaved to sin and that his soul is dead (which is the wages of sin), "living death" captures the essence of mankind better than "deadly life." The dramatic descriptions of his inner struggles which preceded his definite conversion depict with inimitable literary force the practical reality of his philosophical position.[43]

The bondage of the will is a teaching present also in Augustine's early works, although not in the developed form that we read in his later works. A proper treatment of his early works requires its own space and it is not the main focus of this research. What is important to mention here is that, on the one hand, it is true that Augustine's teaching of man's will changed and developed over time. On the other hand, it is even more true that the *seminal* principle of the bondage of the will, with its defining characteristics, is a position that Augustine consistently held from the beginning to the end of his Christian life. The author does not share a common interpretation of the development of Augustine's philosophy. A number of scholars believe that Augustine experienced a radical revolution of his thought around the 390's, witnessed especially by his work *To Simplician, On Various Questions* (397). Independently of the differences among them, these scholars claim that before this period, Augustine was more inclined toward the classic idea of intellectual perfectionism according to

---

42. Augustine, *Confessions*, 1.1.1.

43. "Who am I, and what is my nature? How evil have not my deeds been; or if not my deeds, my words; or if not my words, my will? But You, O Lord, art good and merciful, and Your right hand had respect unto the profoundness of my death, and removed from the bottom of my heart that abyss of corruption. And this was the result, that I willed not to do what I willed, and willed to do what you willed. But where, during all those years, and out of what deep and secret retreat was my free will summoned forth in a moment, whereby I gave my neck to Your "easy yoke," and my shoulders to Your "light burden" (Matt 11:30) O Christ Jesus, 'my strength and my Redeemer'?" *Ibid.*, 9.1.1. Book 13 contains the most explicit description that Augustine offers of the struggles with his will. It is necessary reading in order properly to evaluate the *a posteriori* meditation that Augustine makes in book 9.

which man's will retains an essential inner power to believe in God and do good apart from God's gracious work. After this period, Augustine supposedly modified his theology in a radical way, and started to espouse the total inability of the will to believe in God and to do good and the total dependence of man on God. One of the most famous instances of this interpretation can be found in the excellent biography of Augustine written by Peter Brown, especially the chapter entitled "The Lost Future."[44]

Through a close and systematic reading of the texts, Carol Harrison[45] has proved the continuity of Augustine's theology starting from the very moment of his conversion in 386 to the end of his life. Harrison refutes any theory of intellectual or theological "revolution," without at the same time denying the evident development of Augustine's thinking. According to the popular conception, Augustine's conviction of the possible perfect moral life was strongly influenced by his knowledge of classical philosophy and culture. Nevertheless, after studying the Scripture and after meditating on Biblical subjects such as sin and predestination, Augustine renounced his philosophical ideal of perfection in favor of a more dramatic view of man's nature, with a strong belief in the absolute necessity of divine grace in the field of spirituality and morality. This view is ably refuted by Harrison.

On Free Will is one of the Augustinian works often mentioned as evidence for the claim that Augustine, at the beginning of his conversion, held to a more optimistic view of the will and its power. However, a careful reading of *On Free Will*, with Augustine's self-interpretation in *Retractions* 1.9, appears to tell quite a different story (I am mentioning only this work because this is the early writing of Augustine in which he most explicitly discusses the topic of this chapter, i.e., man's will). Harrison has offered a detailed analysis of *On Free Will*.[46] It is important to note that neither Harrison nor any other modern scholar is the first in history to answer and refute the objections that many make against the consistency and continuity of Augustine's thought. Almost five centuries ago, John

---

44. "Augustine, indeed, had decided that he would never reach the fulfilment that he first thought was promised to him by a Christian Platonism: he would never impose a victory of mind over body in himself, he would never achieve the wrapt contemplation of the ideal philosopher. It is the most drastic change that a man may have to accept: it involved nothing less than the surrender of the bright future he thought he had gained at Cassiciacum." Brown, *Augustine of Hippo*, 147. For other similar views, see Lettieri, *L'altro Agostino*; Ferrari, *The Conversions of Saint Augustine*; Fredriksen, "Paul and Augustine: Conversion Narratives, Orthodox Traditions, and Retrospective Self."

45. Harrison, *Rethinking Augustine's Early Theology*.

46. Harrison, *Rethinking Augustine's Early Theology*, 198–226.

Calvin (1509–1564) answered the same points in his *On the Bondage and Liberation of the Will* (1543). Calvin says that Augustine's aim in *On Free Will* "was to show that the origin of sin derived from man's voluntary fall, not from God's act of creation."[47] Calvin also understood that the African theologian "is not discussing what the human will is like now, but what it was like when it was made by God" and that "those remarks which glorify our nature so much referred not to its corrupt state but to when it was still innocent."[48] The French reformer also establishes an interpretative principle which is vitally important: "the author itself . . . certainly ought to have the right to interpret what he has said."[49] If we allow Augustine to explain himself, we will see that in his dialogue *On Free Will* he never intended to defend a doctrine of the ethical liberty of man's will.

Harrison makes basically the same points, when she writes that Augustine "was fully persuaded from the beginning that, if we do not acknowledge our complete and absolute dependence upon God's grace we will be overcome by the ignorance and difficulties that we now suffer, but that, if we humbly accept God's grace, at work both outwardly and inwardly, we will be empowered and enabled to know and to will the good."[50] Moreover, Harrison adds that this humble acceptance of God's grace is not something neutrally in man's power, but it is "a response which is possible only because of the *prior action and gift of grace.*"[51] A global and contextualized reading of *On Free Will* and *Retractions* 1.9 seems to confirm the conclusions of Calvin and Harrison.[52]

The question may be asked: if Augustine's position on man's will remained basically the same from his conversion until the end of his life, why does he talk about *On Free Will* in *Retractions* 1.9? Why does Augustine correct his own work? Augustine himself gives us the answer in two places, and the answer seems to be as follows: Pelagius took some sections of Augustine's *On Free Will*, quoted them out of context, and then abused them to claim that Augustine had in the past held the same position that Pelagius was espousing. Augustine was compelled to answer this claim of Pelagius.[53] In *Retractions* 1.9 and *On Nature and Grace* 67.80–81,

47. Calvin, *The Bondage and the Liberation of the Will*, 90–96.

48. *Ivi.*

49. *Ivi.*

50. Harrison, *Rethinking Augustine's Early Theology*, 223.

51. *Ibid.*, 220.

52. For additional similar interpretations, see Madec, *La Patrie et la Voi*; Cipriani, "Le fonti cristiane della dottrina trinitaria nei primi Dialoghi di s. Agostino," 253–312.

53. Augustine, *Retractions*, 1.9, especially 1.9.5; *On Nature and Grace*, 67.80–81.

Augustine explains and contextualizes those sections that Pelagius used to
support his doctrine of the freedom of the will.

In *Retractions* 1.9 Augustine himself quotes several passages from
this early dialogue to show that, also at that time, he believed in the absolute necessity of divine help. This is one of them: "But, though man fell
through his own will, he cannot rise through his own will. Therefore let
us believe firmly that God's right hand, that is, Our Lord Jesus Christ, is
extended out to us from on high; let us await this help with sure hope, and
let us desire it with ardent charity."[54] Moreover, let us read what Augustine says near the end of his dialogue, which should put an end to every
dispute: "When we speak of a will free to act rightly, we speak of the will
with which man was created."[55] This assertion fits the main purpose of this
dialogue. In fact, the main concern of Augustine was to refute the denial
of free will by Manichaean dualism,[56] and the sections where he explores
the power of the will refer to the human will *before* the fall into sin, when
man actually had a free will, and not *after* the fall, when man lost his free
will. As for Pelagianism (which went to the other extreme exceedingly to
praise man's will), Augustine insists that his *On Free Will*, far from being
on their side, it is actually against them.[57] In fact, in the dialogue it was
clearly stated that all good things come from God. The good use of the
will is among these good things. Therefore, the good use of the will is a gift
that only God may grant. Thus, the claim of Pelagius concerning an early
Augustinian belief of a post-fall will that is able to make a free and neutral
choice between good and evil is unfounded.[58]

There is one specific passage of this work that is particularly enlightening about Augustine's early position of man's nature and man's power of
the will.

> Well, surely that punishment should not be thought a light one,
> which consists in the mind being ruled by passion, being robbed
> of its store of virtue, being dragged hither and thither, poor and

54. Augustine, *On Free Will*, 2.20.54, quoted in Augustine, *Retractions*, 1.9.4.

55. Augustine, *On Free Will*, 3.18.52.

56. "This disputation is to be considered as directed against the Manicheans, who
do not accept the Scripture of the Old Testament, where an account of original sin is
given, and who maintain, with detestable arrogance, that what is read about it in the
apostolic writings was interpolated by corrupters of the Scriptures, as though it has not
been said by the apostles themselves." Augustine, *Retractions* 1.9.6.

57. "Observe how long before the Pelagian heresy had come into existence we spoke
as though we were already speaking against them." *Ivi.*

58. *Ivi.*

needy, now judging false for true, now defending, now attacking what before it approved, and in spite of this running off into fresh falsehood, now withholding its assent, and often frightened of clear reasoning, now despairing of finding any truth at all, and clinging closely to the darkness of its folly, now striving for the light of understanding, and again falling back through exhaustion.

Meanwhile the passions rage like tyrants, and throw into confusion the whole soul and life of men with storms from every quarter, fear on one side, desire on another, on another anxiety, or false empty joy, here pain for the thing which was loved and lost, there eagerness to win what is not possessed, there grief for an injury received, here burning desire to avenge it. Wherever he turns, avarice can confine him, self-indulgence dissipate him, ambition master him, pride puff him up, envy torture him, sloth drug him, obstinacy rouse him, oppression afflict him, and the countless other feelings which crowd and exploit the power of passion. Can we then think this no punishment at all, which, as you see, all who do not cling to wisdom must necessarily suffer?[59]

This quote is rather interesting because it represents one of Augustine's first detailed description of the effects of sin on man, both from an *intellectual* and an *ethical* point of view. Here is the circular reference to epistemology and ethics. In fact, the first section of the citation talks primarily about the condition of man's *mind*, while the second section is focused on the condition of man's *morality*. Augustine says that the punishment resulting from the fall of mankind into sin has affected both departments of man's being. Even though Augustine does not divide the two spheres, he seems to assert that the intellectual or epistemological errors are caused by the *ethical* problem. In fact, because "the mind" is "ruled by passion, being robbed of its store of virtue" (a distinctively ethical problem) man judges "false for true" and his reason commits the mistakes that the passage mentions. Ethics has a certain priority inasmuch as both the moral errors and the intellectual errors are grounded in an *ethical* problem. It is true that the "passions rage like tyrants, and throw into confusion the whole soul and life of men" because they are the results of wrong deliberations of the mind, but this mind deliberates erroneously because of its ethical flaw. This means that the punishment of sin upon man is so great and deep that it overwhelms the whole of man's existence. In light of this condition, for

59. Augustine, *On Free Will*, 2.11.22.

Augustine it does not follow that man has a free will able to make a neutral choice between good and evil. This free will, and its good use, comes from God alone.[60]

In light of these considerations, Brown's assertion according to which the early Augustine was "more Pelagian than Pelagius"[61] is unfounded, and the interpretation of Calvin and Harrison (which I support) is correct. However, both to give a fair account of Brown's position and to support further the point discussed here, it is appropriate to report what Brown himself says in the chapter entitled "New Directions" contained in the second edition of his superb work. After the discovery of some new sermons and letters by Augustine, Brown rejected his earlier interpretation of a philosophically optimistic young Augustine as opposed to a theologically dour elderly Augustine. This is what Brown says: "Central elements in Augustine's thought have been shown to be remarkably stable. They seem to bear little trace of discontinuity. Augustine's intellectual life as a bishop cannot be said to have been lived out entirely in the shadow of a 'Lost Future,' as I had suggested in the chapter of my book which bears that title. In the same manner, the latter decades of Augustine's thought on grace, free will and predestination cannot be highly dismissed as the departure of a tired old man from the view of an earlier, 'better' self. As a thinker, Augustine was, perhaps, more a man *aus einem Guss*, all of a piece, and less riven by fateful discontinuities than I had thought."[62]

The reason why I have mentioned Brown's earlier interpretation as representative of the interpretation of a "revolution" in Augustine's thought is that his masterful biography of Augustine has influenced an entire generation of Augustinian scholars.[63] Therefore, the quote above is certainly quite an interesting statement from a scholar who has written one of the most important works on Augustine.

On the subject of the will and its supposed liberty, the similarities between Augustine and Luther are so great and evident that Luther in his major work, *The Bondage of the Will*, does not hesitate to affirm that, regarding the subject of the will, Augustine held essentially his same

60. *Ibid.*, 2.20.54.

61. "Augustine was, on paper, more Pelagian than Pelagius." Brown, *Augustine*, 148. With "more Pelagian than Pelagius," Brown means that the young African thinker had a conception of the will even more radical than Pelagius, that is, that the young Augustine believed in the freedom of the will in the fields of spirituality and morality.

62. *Ibid*, 490.

63. "Our Augustine is Brown's." J. J. O'Donnell, "The Next Life of Augustine."

position.[64] This was not an hyperbolic or rhetorical statement. An unbiased reading of the works of the African thinker easily shows that Luther's claim is accurate. If I should quote all the passages from the works of Augustine that explain his teaching regarding man and free will and that show his agreement with Luther, this chapter would become excessively long. The comparison made here has been the easiest to make, considering the evident agreement between the two authors on this subject. Another Augustinian reformer whom I consider an even better developer of Augustine's thought than Luther is John Calvin, already mentioned above. On the subject of the will, Calvin was in great agreement with Luther. In fact, he argues that Augustine "is certainly on our side,"[65] the same claim that Luther makes in *The Bondage of the Will*. As a matter of fact, Calvin wrote his book on man's will also as an apology not only of his own teaching but also of Martin Luther's, whom he openly mentions and highly esteems.

In addition to what has been said, even if this interpretation of Augustine's *On Free Will* should be wrong, there is an interpretative element that gives the final blow to any claim of a libertarian position of the African theologian: Augustine's later works cannot be interpreted in light of Augustine's earlier works. For the sake of argument, let us say that the young Augustine was in favour of the doctrine of a sort of moral freedom of the will. Even in this case, this would not disprove that Augustine's most proper and mature position is that of the moral necessity and bondage of man's will. This is because Augustine's thought was a *development*. As such, Augustine gradually perfected it, changing theological details and refining his exegesis. This can be easily deduced from what Augustine himself says about his own intellectual progression: "I freely confess, accordingly, that I endeavour to be one of those who write because they have made some progress, and who, by means of writing, make further progress."[66] In light

---

64. ". . . Augustine . . . is entirely with me." Luther, *The Bondage of the Will*, 109. This assertion has to be read in its context: Augustine is "entirely" with Luther on the topics discussed on his *On Free Will*, i.e., the will and related issues. However, it is also true that Luther sees his agreement with Augustine also on other essential issues, such as God's omnipotence and grace, election and predestination.

65. Calvin, *The Bondage and the Liberation of the Will*, 100. Calvin repeats the same concept in other places of the same book, as well as in his major work, *Institutes of The Christian Religion*, 2.2.4–9; 2.3.13–14. Calvin, more than Luther, also rightly boasts about the harmony between Augustine and himself on predestination (see his *God's Eternal Predestination and Secret Providence*), though it is the opinion of the present writer that Calvin sets forth a better and more logical development of the Augustinian theology of grace from an exegetical and systematic point of view.

66. Augustine, *Letters*, 143.2.

of the description that Augustine himself gives of his own position, the least that an Augustinian scholar may do is to trust his words, and not interpret the more developed later works in light of the less developed earlier works, not only concerning the seemingly controversial issues as the ones that are the focus of this research, but also concerning his philosophy as a whole. This means that, to understand Augustine's final position, the statements of the works of his earlier years which are supposedly in support of a libertarian view of the will should be interpreted and regulated by the doctrinal statements that we find in his later works, and not vice-versa. Therefore, since the later Augustine clearly taught a doctrine of moral necessity and total spiritual inability of the will, this makes that doctrine Augustine's most genuine and complete position on the issue. We can also see this in Augustine's recollection of his study of the issue of the will over time, with which we close this analysis: "In the solution of this question I, indeed, labored in defense of the free choice of the human will, *but the grace of God conquered*, and finally I was able to understand, with full clarity, the meaning of the Apostle, 'For who singles thee out? Or what hast thou that thou hast not received? But if thou hast received it, why dost thou boast as if thou hadst not received it?' (1 Cor 4:7)."[67]

This analysis of Augustine's earlier doctrine of the will has been conducted in order to show the genuine Augustinianism of Luther's *Heidelberg Disputation*. Luther's doctrine of the bondage of the will is coherently grounded on Augustine's theological anthropology of the moral necessity of the will, an anthropology that Augustine believed (and developed) during his life. As has been noted, this chapter, with the other chapters of comparison, is subservient to what will be said in the fifth chapter and in the conclusion that constitutes the philosophical core of this book. In this chapter we have seen that the Augustinian philosophy of man takes its first principles from a Biblical view of man. It has a most honest approach: the first principles of a philosophy, according to the most basic logic, cannot be demonstrated, but are chosen. According to this view, man is morally corrupt. As a result of his willful and conscious fall into sin, man has become unable to do or to wish good with his own strength or will. This does not mean that every single man *actually* commits all possible evil, but that he is *potentially* able to commit it. Moreover, the focus is not primarily on what man does or may do, but on what man *is*. His will is not free. This does not mean that he is compelled to sin, but rather that he cannot do anything other than willingly and consciously sin, and this is

67. Augustine, *Retractions*, 1.9.6.

because of the guilt of the first man legally and spiritually extended to all his descendants. Man's will, although still present, has been enslaved and taken captive to sin by its willful and conscious choice.

However, if this is the truth about man and his will, how is it possible to reach the so-called "good life"? How is it possible to be a good person, a moral individual, a well doer, or to fulfill the moral law? It is not possible. It follows that any form of moralism is utterly ruled out by the Christian philosophy of the cross. But these assertions need further explanation. We will now discuss the issue of good works.

CHAPTER 3

THE LAW OF GOD
AND THE WORKS OF MAN

THE SECOND SECTION OF the *Heidelberg Disputation* deals with the essence and the role of the law of God, the Ten Commandments, which was already mentioned but not properly developed in the previous chapter. We have studied the anthropological structure of man, his ethical nature. We have seen that man by nature is totally unable and utterly unwilling to do good because his will has become depraved as a result of man's fall into sin. Most importantly, we have carefully analyzed the Augustinian nature of Luther's theses. The differences between the two are negligible. The second section that we shall analyze will demonstrate in what respect, or with respect to *what*, the will of man is powerless. It is powerless to do good, that is, to fulfill the standard of good established by God. This standard is the law of God, the Ten Commandments. I now let Luther and Augustine speak. Luther begins his treatment of the subject in his usual sharply polemical way.

> *1. The law of God, the most salutary doctrine of life, cannot advance man on his way to righteousness, but rather hinders him.*[1]

1. "This is made clear by the Apostle in his letter to the Romans (3:21): 'But now the righteousness of God has been manifested apart from the law.' St. Augustine interprets this in his book *The Spirit and the Letter* (*De Spiritu et Littera*): 'Without the law, that is, without its support.' In Rom 5:20 the Apostle states, 'Law intervened, to increase the trespass,' and in Rom 7:9 he adds, 'But when the commandment came, sin revived.' For this reason he calls the law 'a law of death' and 'a law of sin' in Rom 8:2. Indeed, in 2

2. Much less can human works, which are done over and over again with the aid of natural precepts, so to speak, lead to that end.[2]

Augustine and Luther do not hold to any autonomous morality of reason.[3] For them, morality is revealed, and it is revealed by the God of Christianity through his law, which can be summarized in the Ten Commandments. From an Augustinian point of view, without God morality is only a plaything for hypocrites. Moreover, it is necessary to explain briefly the ethical requirements and implications of this law.

According to Augustine, the law of God is perfect and holy, as God is perfect and holy. Since both the law and the Lawgiver are perfectly holy, man must fulfil this law with perfect holiness. God is not satisfied with "our best effort," which may fit well into a subjective, comfortable morality like the ethics of Kant, but which will not satisfy the God of Christianity who demands perfect obedience to his law. In addition to this, obedience must be accomplished in a state of perfect love for God.[4] Now, we have already seen that man is neither perfect nor holy. On the contrary, he is morally sinful and spiritually depraved. This means that he cannot honor and satisfy the requirements of the law of God, which can be summarized as follows: "Thou shalt love the Lord thy God with all thy heart, and with all thy soul, and with all thy mind, and with all thy strength: this is the

------

Cor 3:6 he says, 'the written code kills,' which St. Augustine throughout his book *The Spirit and the Letter* understands as applying to every law, even the holiest law of God." Luther, *Heidelberg*, Proof 1.

2. "Since the law of God, which is holy and unstained, true, just, etc., is given man by God as an aid beyond his natural powers to enlighten him and move him to do the good, and nevertheless the opposite takes place, namely, that he becomes more wicked, how can he, left to his own power and without such aid, be induced to do good? If a person does not do good with help from without, he will do even less by his own strength. Therefore the Apostle, in Rom 3:10–12, calls all persons corrupt and impotent who neither understand nor seek God, for all, he says, have gone astray." *Ibid.*, Proof 2.

3. "Today when secularists praise reason, they do not mean what Augustine, Descartes and Spinoza meant by *reason*. These three men meant an intellectual ability to argue. The secularists are (almost unanimously in this twentieth century) empiricists, and by *reason* they mean sensory experience." Clark, *Logic*, 8. The same can be said of Luther. The German thinker never despises *reason* properly defined as the proper use of the rules of logic.

4. This concept is present both in the Old Testament ("Cursed be he that confirmeth not all the words of this law to do them." Deut 27:26) and in the New Testament ("For whosoever shall keep the whole law, and yet offend in one point, he is guilty of all." Jas 2:10).

first commandment . . . Thou shalt love thy neighbour as thyself" (Mark 12:30–31).

As a result, the law of God "cannot advance man on his way to righteousness, but rather hinders him," or, to use the words of Augustine, "the knowledge of the law makes a proud transgressor."[5] God's law, although good, has become in a sense an "enemy" of man, or, better, man has become the enemy of God's law. At the same time, though, it is also a friend, because the law "by terrifying leads to faith. Thus certainly the law works wrath, that the mercy of God may bestow grace on the sinner, frightened and turned to the fulfillment of the righteousness of the law through Jesus Christ our Lord."[6] Nevertheless, man usually believes that the law is the moral end in itself, which turns what is in itself good into a curse "since the knowledge of the law, unless it be accompanied by the assistance of grace, rather avails for producing the transgression of the commandment."[7]

We repeat that there is nothing wrong with the demands of God's law. This law is, basically, the Ten Commandments, and Luther places particular emphasis on the first one because it encloses and develops in itself all the others. Nevertheless, to use Luther's expression, man is so "curved"[8] upon himself that he cannot do anything but seek "himself in everything" that he does, even when he tries to honor the law of God. The first thing that Luther is concerned to clarify is that "the law of God" is "the most salutary doctrine of life." We now discover that man's will has become so corrupt that even when he tries to fulfill this law, his effort does not improve him in righteousness but rather it draws him further away from righteousness. Luther reveals the Augustinian character of his assertion, pointing to *The Spirit and the Letter* in proof 6.

We must keep in mind that, even though the two philosophers are referring mainly and primarily to the law of God, by implication this principle extends to any kind of law. At least, this is the interpretation that Luther gives of Augustine: "St. Augustine throughout his book *The Spirit and the Letter* understands as applying to every law, even the holiest law of

---

5. Augustine, *Against Two Letters of the Pelagians*, 4.5.11.

6. *Ibid.*

7. Augustine, *On the Grace of Christ and on Original Sin*, 1.9.

8. "Due to our original sin, our nature is so curved in upon itself at its deepest levels that it not only bends the best gifts of God toward itself in order to enjoy them (as the moralists [*iustitiarii*, 'workmongers'] and hypocrites make evident), nay, rather, 'uses' God in order to obtain them, but it does not even know that, in this wicked, twisted crooked way, it seeks everything, including God, only for itself." Luther, *Romans*, 159, on Romans 5:4. For a similar concept of *curvitas* in Augustine, see *The City of God*, 22.22.2; *Expositions on the Psalms*, 37.10.

God." Augustine and Luther believe that the highest law (the law of God), even though good in itself, by itself cannot give to man salvation or moral advancement. By implication, this inability must be true of all other lower laws, be they civil or spiritual.

What Luther means in thesis 1 is that the mere external practice of the law, so called "good works," is powerless and without any positive value in the eyes of God. Luther quotes *The Spirit and the Letter* 9.15, in which passage Augustine discusses the Epistle of the Apostle Paul to the Romans.[9] Like Luther, Augustine rejects that interpretation according to which the law only tells us what to do and, once we know our duty before God, we are able to do that by a free determination of our own will. Augustine argues that Paul "does not say, the righteousness of man, or the righteousness of his own will, but '*the righteousness of God*,'— not that whereby He is Himself righteous, but that with which He endows man when He justifies the ungodly."[10] The African theologian thus teaches that man cannot be righteous by himself. Instead, man's righteousness is external. It is the gift of righteousness, given from the one Lawgiver who establishes what is righteous and what is not. It is heteronomous righteousness. Luther says that righteousness is received independently of any kind of laws or regulations, including God's law. Augustine makes the same point in the passage quoted by Luther: "That righteousness of God, however, is without the law, which God by the Spirit of grace bestows on the believer without the help of the law—that is, when not helped by the law."[11] Augustine affirms that the only true righteousness, the righteousness of God (intended not as his attribute, but as that righteousness that he freely gives to the sinner) has been revealed apart from the law, that is, not merely independently of the law as such, but independently of the *support* of the law of God. The law is, in fact, good and worthy to be honoured, but in itself it has no saving power whatsoever for man: on the contrary, any attempt to be righteous through repeated works obtains the opposite, namely, that man becomes more wicked, as the following theses assert.

---

9. "Therefore by the deeds of the law there shall no flesh be justified in his sight: for by the law is the knowledge of sin. But now the righteousness of God without the law is manifested, being witnessed by the law and the prophets; Even the righteousness of God which is by faith of Jesus Christ unto all and upon all them that believe: for there is no difference." Rom 3:20–22.

10. Augustine, *The Spirit and the Letter*, 9.15.

11. *Ivi.* See also *The Spirit and the Letter*, 14.23–25. See the following chapter for a more detailed treatment of this important point.

3. Although the works of man always seem attractive and good, they are nevertheless likely to be mortal sins.[12]

4. Although the works of God are always unattractive and appear evil, they are nevertheless really eternal merits.[13]

Theses 3 and 4 are an example of the typical method that Luther often employed in order to express Christian truth: by *contrast*, or opposition. According to Luther, truth reveals itself *sub contra specie*, under opposite appearances. This is true not only with respect to truth and the knowledge of the truth as such, but also with respect to a consideration of the way God saves His elect.[14] Truth always reveals itself in the *opposite* manner

12. "Human works appear attractive outwardly, but within they are filthy, as Christ says concerning the Pharisees in Matt 23:27. For they appear to the doer and others good and beautiful, yet God does not judge according to appearances but searches 'the minds and hearts' (Ps 7:9). For without grace and faith it is impossible to have a pure heart. Acts 15:9: 'He cleansed their hearts by faith.' The thesis is proven in the following way: If the works of righteous men are sins, as Thesis 7 of this disputation states, this is much more the case concerning the works of those who are not righteous. But the just speak in behalf of their works in the following way: 'Do not enter into judgment with thy servant, Lord, for no man living is righteous before thee' (Ps 143:2). The Apostle speaks likewise in Gal 3:10, 'All who rely on the works of the law are under the curse.' But the works of men are the works of the law, and the curse will not be placed upon venial sins. Therefore they are mortal sins. In the third place, Rom 2:21 states, 'You who teach others not to steal, do you steal?' St. Augustine interprets this to mean that men are thieves according to their guilty consciences even if they publicly judge or reprimand other thieves." Luther, *Heidelberg*, Proof 3.

13. "That the works of God are unattractive is clear from what is said in Isa 53:2, 'He had no form of comeliness,' and in 1 Sam 2:6, 'The Lord kills and brings to life; he brings down to Sheol and raises up.' This is understood to mean that the Lord humbles and frightens us by means of the law and the sight of our sins so that we seem in the eyes of men, as in our own, as nothing, foolish, and wicked, for we are in truth that. Insofar as we acknowledge and confess this, there is 'no form or beauty' in us, but our life is hidden in God (i.e. in the bare confidence in his mercy), finding in ourselves nothing but sin, foolishness, death, and hell, according to that verse of the Apostle in 2 Cor 6:9–10, 'As sorrowful, yet always rejoicing; as dying, and behold we live.' And that it is which Isa 28:21 calls the 'alien work' of God 'that he may do his work' (that is, he humbles us thoroughly, making us despair, so that he may exalt us in his mercy, giving us hope), just as Hab 3:2 states, 'In wrath remember mercy.' Such a man therefore is displeased with all his works; he sees no beauty, but only his depravity. Indeed, he also does those things which appear foolish and disgusting to others. This depravity, however, comes into being in us either when God punishes us or when we accuse ourselves, as 1 Cor 11:31 says, 'If we judged ourselves truly, we should not be judged by the Lord.' Deut 32:36 also states, 'The Lord will vindicate his people and have compassion on his servants.' In this way, consequently, the unattractive works which God does in us, that is, those which are humble and devout, are really eternal, for humility and fear of God are our entire merit." *Ibid.*, Proof 4.

14. "For our good is hidden and that so deeply that it is hidden under its opposite.

that man expects. Luther takes this principle from several Scriptural passages, especially 1 Cor 1:20–31.[15] In this passage, Paul teaches that God, in *opposition* to the expectation of a typical wise Gentile, purposely determined to show his *wisdom* in the *foolishness* (notice the *opposite* terms) of a crucified man who claimed to be God incarnate and who was raised three days after his death.[16] In the same way, God purposed to show his *power* through the *weakness* of the *scandal* of a crucified Saviour, in *opposition* to the expectation of a political earthly deliverer that many Jews were expecting at that time. Of course, Paul did not mean to say that the message he was preaching, the preaching of Christ crucified, is scandal and foolishness *in itself*, but in relation to fallen man. Man is sinful, while God is holy. The spiritually weak and miserable man wants that *power* and *glory* that he does not deserve; the holy God in his word forsook the power and glory that were with him from eternity in order to become *weak* and *humble*. Therefore, man always wants and expects the *opposite* of what God has actually planned for his salvation.

The *sub contra specie* principle is mainly evident in God and in his revelation throughout history. The God of Luther is a hidden God, *Deus*

Thus our life is hidden under death, self-love under self-hatred, glory under shame, salvation under perdition, the kingdom under banishment, heaven under hell, wisdom under foolishness, righteousness under sin, strength under weakness. And generally any yes we say to any good under a no, in order that our faith may be anchored in God." Luther, *Romans*, 264.

15. "Where is the wise? where is the scribe? where is the disputer of this world? hath not God made foolish the wisdom of this world? For after that in the wisdom of God the world by wisdom knew not God, it pleased God by the foolishness of preaching to save them that believe. For the Jews require a sign, and the Greeks seek after wisdom: But we preach Christ crucified, unto the Jews a stumblingblock, and unto the Greeks foolishness; But unto them which are called, both Jews and Greeks, Christ the power of God, and the wisdom of God. Because the foolishness of God is wiser than men; and the weakness of God is stronger than men. For ye see your calling, brethren, how that not many wise men after the flesh, not many mighty, not many noble, are called: But God hath chosen the foolish things of the world to confound the wise; and God hath chosen the weak things of the world to confound the things which are mighty; And base things of the world, and things which are despised, hath God chosen, yea, and things which are not, to bring to nought things that are: That no flesh should glory in his presence. But of him are ye in Christ Jesus, who of God is made unto us wisdom, and righteousness, and sanctification, and redemption: That, according as it is written, He that glorieth, let him glory in the Lord." 1 Cor 1:21–30.

16. The Book of Acts 17:32 reports that, on the occasion of Paul's speech to the Areopagus in Athens, the assembled crowd started to mock the apostle when he mentioned the Christian idea of resurrection. Among these, there were some Epicurean and Stoic philosophers.

absconditus.[17] Luther's *sub contra specie* and the hiddenness of God are two concepts strictly related to each other. God is hidden because he has determined to reveal his *power* and *wisdom* under the opposite appearances (*sub contra specie*) of the *weakness* and *foolishness* of the cross. While everybody was expecting Christ to substantiate his claim to be God in the flesh through a sign of political power and earthly wisdom, he actually demonstrated his claims through the foolish and humiliating death of the cross. Even more absurd, this show of weakness and foolishness is supposed to be not only *a* revelation of God, but his *highest* revelation: "In this way he [God] acted in his proper work, in that which is the foremost of his works and the pattern of all of them, i.e., in Christ. When he wanted to glorify him, he made him die, he caused him to be confounded and to descend into hell, contrary in the utmost to what all his disciples fervently wished and hoped in their devoutest thoughts."[18]

These are the reasons why Luther expresses himself using paradoxes. Both with his language and with his ideas, Luther wants to contradict human ethical expectations, just as God contradicts human expectations when he reveals himself. It is important to add that by "paradox" is not intended a truth or an idea that is paradoxical or logically contradictory *in itself*. A paradox in this context is a concept that *appears* impossible to natural man apart from God's enlightenment. The epistemological problem is found not in the constitution of the truth as such, but in the epistemological principles of man and, especially, in his ethical nature.

Before discussing the Augustinian nature of theses 3 and 4 as such, there are few important questions to ask: Do we find a similar hermeneutical and epistemological principle also in Augustine? If this is the case, does Augustine take it from Scripture? Does the truth reveal itself *sub contra specie* also for Augustine? There are several passages that seem to suggest the presence of a similar principle in the works of Augustine. Augustine, who is clearly the origin of the Lutheran version, applies his principle to the interpretation of Scripture, as well as to the revelation of God throughout history and to the work of providence and redemption.

17. Luther takes this expression from the Latin Vugalte Bible, Isa 45:15: "vere tu es Deus absconditus Deus Israhel salvator."

18. Luther, *Romans*, 242. Interestingly, in the same passage Luther continues as follows: "So he [God] dealt with Blessed Augustine, when he let him fall deeper and deeper into error despite the prayer of his mother, so that he might grant it to her beyond her asking. And so he deals with all saints." *Ivi*.

In *On Christian Doctrine* 1.14.13,[19] Augustine explains the redemption worked by Christ according to this epiphanic structure. The general context of this section is the art of interpreting Scripture, that is, exegesis. The specific context is an analysis of the redemptive method that God uses to heal mankind by his saving work. Augustine says that the history of redemption is a gradual process of healing of mankind. The wisdom of God sometimes heals man's wounds by their "likes," and sometimes by their "opposites." The clearest of these opposites is the fact that mankind has been ensnared by the apparent *wisdom* of the devil, but is healed by the apparent *foolishness* of God. They are "apparent" because, for Augustine God's truth appears to fallen man as *foolishness* even though in itself it is actually wise and rational. Similarly, falsehood appears to fallen man as *wisdom* even though it is actually foolishness: "just as the former [the wisdom of the devil] was called wisdom, but was in reality the folly of those who despised God, so the latter [the foolishness of God] is called foolishness, but is true wisdom in those who overcome the devil."[20] Also here, it must not be concluded that for Augustine God's wisdom is foolishness *in itself*. For both Luther and Augustine, divine wisdom is the only real criterion for truth and rationality. Rather, God's wisdom *appears* as foolishness to *fallen man*. Being at ethical enmity with God, fallen man always contradicts divine revelation, as divine revelation always contradicts fallen man. When God reveals his truth, man always expects the *opposite*.

19. "Just as surgeons, when they bind up wounds, do it not in a slovenly way, but carefully, that there may be a certain degree of neatness in the binding, in addition to its mere usefulness, so our medicine, Wisdom, was by His assumption of humanity adapted to our wounds, curing some of them by their opposites, some of them by their likes . . . the Wisdom of God in healing man has applied Himself to his cure, being Himself healer and medicine both in one. Seeing, then, that man fell through pride, He restored him through humility. *We were ensnared by the wisdom of the serpent: we are set free by the foolishness of God. Moreover, just as the former was called wisdom, but was in reality the folly of those who despised God, so the latter is called foolishness, but is true wisdom in those who overcome the devil.* We used our immortality so badly as to incur the penalty of death: Christ used His mortality so well as to restore us to life. The disease was brought in through a woman's corrupted soul: the remedy came through a woman's virgin body. To the same class of opposite remedies it belongs, that our vices are cured by the example of His virtues. On the other hand, the following are, as it were, bandages made in the same shape as the limbs and wounds to which they are applied: He was born of a woman to deliver us who fell through a woman: He came as a man to save us who are men, as a mortal to save us who are mortals, by death to save us who were dead. And those who can follow out the matter more fully, who are not hurried on by the necessity of carrying out a set undertaking, will find many other points of instruction in considering the remedies, whether opposites or likes, employed in the medicine of Christianity." Augustine, *On Christian Doctrine*, 1.14.13. Emphasis added.

20. *Ivi.*

For this reason the wisdom of the cross of Christ appears foolishness to the Greeks and scandal to the Jews.

In *The City of God*, we may find a few passages that seem to point further to the Augustinian origin of Luther's *sub contra specie* principle. Here Augustine applies his own *sub contra specie* principle not only to the particular work of redemption in Christ, but also to the more general works of creation and providence. More specifically, Augustine is posing a metaphysical question: how can the harmony of creation and providence be maintained by God in spite of the presence of wicked wills in His creation? Augustine answers that "even the wicked will is a strong proof of the goodness of the nature."[21] More important to our discussion, Augustine appeals to the providential and causative foreknowledge of God who "as He is the supremely good Creator of good natures, so is He of evil wills the most just Ruler; so that, while they make an ill use of good natures, He makes a good use even of evil wills."[22] God has predisposed this dialectic of *antithesis* of good and evil throughout history in order to show in a clearer way how even evil in the world will serve God's final good purpose. Thus God composes a metaphysical artwork or, to use Augustine's words, "an exquisite poem set off with antitheses."[23] In this way, God leads history in order that what is good, righteous and true may shine more vividly through the *opposition* of what is evil, unrighteous, and false: "these oppositions of contraries lend beauty to the language, so the beauty of the

21. Augustine, *The City of God*, 11.17.

22. *Ivi.*

23. "For God would never have created any, I do not say angel, but even man, whose future wickedness He foreknew, unless He had equally known to what uses in behalf of the good He could turn him, thus embellishing the course of the ages, as it were an exquisite poem set off with antitheses. For what are called antitheses are among the most elegant of the ornaments of speech. They might be called in Latin 'oppositions,' or, to speak more accurately, 'contrapositions;' but this word is not in common use among us, though the Latin, and indeed the languages of all nations, avail themselves of the same ornaments of style. In the Second Epistle to the Corinthians the Apostle Paul also makes a graceful use of antithesis, in that place where he says, '*By the armor of righteousness on the right hand and on the left, by honor and dishonor, by evil report and good report: as deceivers, and yet true; as unknown, and yet well known; as dying, and, behold, we live; as chastened, and not killed; as sorrowful, yet always rejoicing; as poor, yet making many rich; as having nothing, and yet possessing all things*' (2 Cor 6:7–10). As, then, these oppositions of contraries lend beauty to the language, so the beauty of the course of this world is achieved by the opposition of contraries, arranged, as it were, by an eloquence not of words, but of things. This is quite plainly stated in the Book of Ecclesiasticus, in this way: '*Good is set against evil, and life against death: so is the sinner against the godly. So look upon all the works of the Most High, and these are two and two, one against another*' (Sir 33:15)." *Ibid.*, 11.18.

course of this world is achieved by the opposition of contraries, arranged, as it were, by an eloquence not of words, but of things."[24]

Has Luther been inspired by Augustine in the development of his *sub contra specie* principle? We cannot give an answer with full certainty. Nevertheless, the similarities between Luther's *sub contra specie* and Augustine's "contrapositions" seem to be quite evident. But we now return to the content of theses 3 and 4 of the *Heidelberg Disputation*. What has been said regarding the *sub contra specie* of Luther and the "antitheses" or "contrapositions" of Augustine is the introductory reading key to theses 2 and 4 (and for the entire *Heidelberg Disputation* as well). The *sub contra specie* principle is necessary for understanding both the "paradoxical" content and form of the assertions of Luther, with their Augustinian nature.

The *sub contra specie* principle is foundational to theses 3 and 4. Here Luther says that human works appear outwardly attractive. They seem good, but actually they are mortal sins. On the contrary, the works of God always appear unattractive. They seem evil, but actually they are eternal merits. This situation has been caused by the fallen state of man. Because of his sinfulness, man always considers truth as falsity and falsity as true, good as evil and evil as good, holiness as unholiness and unholiness as holiness, foolishness as true wisdom and true wisdom as foolishness. Fallen man's epistemology is inverted because his ethics is inverted, which in turn is inverted because his epistemology is erroneous and unable to give him a true account of his own nature and the needs of his existence. Ethics implies a specific epistemology, and a specific epistemology implies a certain ethics.

Concerning theses 3 and 4, the agreement with Augustine is interesting and striking. We have already discussed passages in which the African theologian states that human works accomplished without grace and faith are actually sins. The present chapter will substantiate even further this claim through an appeal to several Augustinian passages. To begin, it will be interesting to analyze a particular passage, inasmuch as it contains a sort of "contrast" or "contraposition," in line with the paradoxes of Luther.

Augustine gives the example of a man who seems blameless from an external point of view. He "leads his life without murder, without theft, without false-witness, without coveting other men's goods, giving due honour to his parents, chaste even to continence from all carnal intercourse whatever, even conjugal, most liberal in almsgiving, most patient

---

24. *Ivi.* For other Augustinian passages on the subject of "oppositions" or "contrapositions," see *Letters*, 3.20; *Sermons*, 341.4.

of injuries; who not only does not deprive another of his goods, but does not even ask again for what has been taken away from himself; or who has even sold all his own property and appropriated it to the poor, and possesses nothing which belongs to him as his own."[25] According to the natural judgment of man's reason, this man is a perfect example of morality. However, God sees it altogether differently: "if he has not a true and catholic faith in God, must yet depart from this life to condemnation."[26]

As a contrast, Augustine considers a Christian believer who, even though he strives to lead a godly life, also has many struggles in several areas: "he does not, like the other, well refrain altogether, but pays and repays the debt of carnal connection . . . does not receive injuries with so much patience, but is raised into anger with the desire of vengeance, although, in order that he may say, '*As we also forgive our debtors,*' forgives when he is asked—possesses personal property, giving thence indeed some alms, but not as the former so liberally—does not take away what belongs to another, but, although by ecclesiastical, not by civil judgment, yet contends for his own."[27] About such an individual, the reason of man will rush to pronounce the typical accusation that Christians have always faced: hypocrisy. This man calls himself a Christian, but his conduct is inconsistent with his claim: he is a real hypocrite. Yet, even though Augustine does not deny the evident inconsistencies of this believing man, also here, however, the standard of God overturns the arguments, judging the "laudable" unbelieving man as a hypocrite and unrighteous and the believing man who is "inferior in morals" as honest and righteous.

Why is such a criterion so offensive and illogical to man's natural reason? Because the believing man, "who seems so inferior in morals to the former, on account of the right faith which he has in God, by which he lives, and according to which in all his wrong-doings he accuses himself, and in all his good works praises God, giving to himself the shame, to God the glory, and receiving from Him both forgiveness of sins and love of right deeds—shall be delivered for this life, and depart to be received into the company of those who shall reign with Christ."[28] The believing "immoral" man has received that righteousness which is obtained by grace alone through faith alone, which allows him to do good works, as weak and imperfect as they may be. His works are from a faith which "is not a

25. Augustine, *Against Two Letters of the Pelagians*, 3.5.14.
26. Ivi.
27. Ivi.
28. Ivi.

reprobate faith, since it works by love."[29] The unbelieving "moral" man, on the other hand, does not have such faith. Without faith, he does not possess the righteousness of God. Without the righteousness of God which man may possess through faith by grace, "even those things which seem good works are turned into sins: '*For everything which is not of faith is sin*' (Rom 14:23)."[30] And, for Augustine, the main sin is pride. The "moral" unbelieving person of Augustine's example, even though full of "virtues" and "good works," in his *pride* he rejects the highest *humility*, that is Christ, considering his own person an end in itself.[31] This is true for all those who, without faith, think to do good works acceptable to God (as well as those who have faith and think to gain merits because of the inner worth of their supposed good works, as we will see). For Augustine, these individuals are actually performing what Luther calls "mortal sins" because these works are done out of pride, and "it is thus that pride in its perversity apes God."[32] Thus, for Augustine man is absolutely dependent upon God's grace not only for his conversion, but also for a truly virtuous life acceptable to God.[33]

Augustine and Luther not only defend the same concepts, but also the language used to convey their beliefs is similar. They set forth a contrast between what natural man usually judges as good and righteous in opposition to what God judges good and righteous. To use Luther's words of proof 4, the weak but believing man whom Augustine describes sees himself as "nothing, foolish, and wicked," finding in himself "nothing but

29. *Ivi.*

30. *Ivi.*

31. Augustine, *The City of God*, 14,13.1.

32. *Ibid.*, 19.12.2.

33. "For though the soul may seem to rule the body admirably, and the reason the vices, if the soul and reason do not themselves obey God, as God has commanded them to serve Him, they have no proper authority over the body and the vices. For what kind of mistress of the body and the vices can that mind be which is ignorant of the true God, and which, instead of being subject to His authority, is prostituted to the corrupting influences of the most vicious demons? It is for this reason that *the virtues which it seems to itself to possess, and by which it restrains the body and the vices that it may obtain and keep what it desires, are rather vices than virtues so long as there is no reference to God in the matter.* For although some suppose that virtues which have a reference only to themselves, and are desired only on their own account, are yet true and genuine virtues, the fact is that *even then they are inflated with pride, and are therefore to be reckoned vices rather than virtues.* For as that which gives life to the flesh is not derived from flesh, but is above it, so that which gives blessed life to man is not derived from man, but is something above him; and what I say of man is true of every celestial power and virtue whatsoever." *Ibid.*, 19.25. Emphasis added.

sin, foolishness, death, and hell." Or, to use again the parallel words of Augustine, "he accuses himself, and in all his good works praises God, giving to himself the shame, to God the glory."[34] We can now see that the weak believer described by Augustine is the recipient of that divine operation that Luther calls in proof 4 the "alien work" of God: this man, under the operation of the grace of God, is humbled and driven to despair, so that he may be exalted and receive hope. On the other hand, this exaltation of the humbled believer is what Luther calls the proper saving work of God. On the contrary, the works and life of the unbelieving "moral" man "appear to the doer and others good and beautiful," but not to God. Man is satisfied with mere outward appearance. Yet God looks at the very bottom of the heart, and there he does not look for our own righteousness, but for the righteousness that he himself graciously gives through faith.

> 5. *The works of men are thus not mortal sins (we speak of works which are apparently good), as though they were crimes.*[35]

> 6. *The works of God (we speak of those which he does through man) are thus not merits, as though they were sinless.*[36]

Theses 5 and 6 strengthen the contrast of the two preceding theses, together offering another contrast. They explain further what Luther means by "mortal sin." A mortal sin is not only an evident crime punishable by human civil laws. As proof 5 states, mortal sins are also those human works which are intended to be good but which in fact are deadly because they are "essentially fruits of a bad root and a bad tree." Man can

---

34. Augustine, *Against Two Letters of the Pelagians*, 3.5.14.

35. "For crimes are such acts which can also be condemned before men, such as adultery, theft, homicide, slander, etc. Mortal sins, on the other hand, are those which seem good yet are essentially fruits of a bad root and a bad tree. Augustine states this in the fourth book of *Against Julian (Contra Julianum)*." Luther, *Heidelberg*, Proof 5.

36. "In Eccl 7:20, we read, 'Surely there is not a righteous man on earth who does good and never sins.' In this connection, however, some people say that the righteous man indeed sins, but not when he does good. They may be refuted in the following manner: If that is what this verse wants to say, why waste so many words? Or does the Holy Spirit like to indulge in loquacious and foolish babble? For this meaning would then be adequately expressed by the following: 'There is not a righteous man on earth who does not sin.' Why does he add 'who does good,' as if another person were righteous who did evil? For no one except a righteous man does good. Where, however, he speaks of sins outside the realm of good works he speaks thus (Prov 24:16), 'The righteous man falls seven times a day.' Here he does not say: A righteous man falls seven times a day when he does good. This is a comparison: If someone cuts with a rusty and rough hatchet, even though the worker is a good craftsman, the hatchet leaves bad, jagged, and ugly gashes. So it is when God works through us." *Ibid.*, Proof 6.

be as "well-intentioned" as he desires, but as long as he remains a "bad tree" with a "bad root" he cannot but generate bad "fruit." This is because Augustinianism sees the fundamental problem of sin not in mere motivations, but in a degradation of the very nature of man.

Luther sets forth another contrast. He mentions *Against Julian* in the proof of thesis 5. We can see that Luther is correct in claiming the support of Augustine. In fact, Julian of Eclanum (386–455) makes the same mistakes as the theological adversaries of Luther. He judges as good the works of the pagans only because they appear externally good. Augustine answers that Julian is misled by the mere appearance of things and accuses Julian of rejecting the revealed Christian teaching regarding good works.[37] Augustine puts the same focus on the term *seems* as Luther does. The point is not what these deeds *seem* according to man's judgment, but what they actually *are* according to God's judgment as revealed in Scripture.

In thesis 6, Luther specifies that even those who are righteous are still unable to perform "sinless" works, that is, works that are morally perfect. Even though God, who is perfect, is the one who works in them when they do good works, he still works in accordance with the nature of the means he uses, means which are still imperfect. We need to remember that Luther, even more than Augustine, distinguishes *justification* (God *declaring* the believer righteous) from *sanctification* (God gradually and slowly *making* the believer holy), where the first is a completed act while the second is an ongoing, developing process. The two cannot be separated but, at the same time, they must be distinguished. Augustine was also convinced that even the most just men are imperfect and that their works are stained by sin: "whatever be the quality or extent of the righteousness which we may definitely ascribe to the present life, there is not a man living in it who

---

37. "This good of men, this good will, this good work can be conferred on no one without the grace of God which is given through the one Mediator of God and men, and only through this good can man be brought to the eternal gift and kingdom of God. All other works which seem praiseworthy among men may seem to you to be true virtues and they may seem to be good works and to be carried out without any sin, but as for me, I know this: They were not performed by a good will, for an unbelieving and ungodly will is not a good will. You call these wills good trees; it suffices for me that they are barren with God and therefore not good. They may be fruitful with those for whom they are also good, relying on your word, your praise, and, if you like, you as planter; yet, whether you will or no, I shall win my point that the love of the world by which a man is a friend of this world is not from God, and that the love of enjoying any creature whatsoever without love of the Creator is not from God; but the love of God which leads one to God is only from God the Father through Jesus Christ with the Holy Spirit." Augustine, *Against Julian*, 4.3.33.

is absolutely free from all sin."[38] Augustine, therefore, never believed that man could attain moral perfection in this earthly life; indeed, the African theologian declares the imperfection of all good works of the righteous, postponing perfection to the life to come.[39] Moreover, Luther declares that the 'works of God (we speak of those which he does through man) are thus not merits."[40] This phrase of Luther echoes the famous and very beautiful Augustinian expression according to which God will reward our good works not because they are meritorious in themselves, but only because in doing so he is crowning his own gifts in us, which he has freely and graciously bestowed upon us.[41]

Now we have the basis on which analyze the next two theses.

> 7. *The works of the righteous would be mortal sins if they would not be feared as mortal sins by the righteous themselves out of pious fear of God.*[42]

38. Augustine, *The Spirit and the Letter*, 65. See also *On Merit and the Forgiveness of Sins, and the Baptism of Infants*, 1.6.7–7.8; *Enchiridion*, 64.

39. "Let us, as many as are running perfectly, be thus resolved, that, being not yet perfected, we pursue our course to perfection along the way by which we have thus far run perfectly, in order that "when that which is perfect has come, then that which is in part may be done away" (1 Cor 13:10) that is, may cease to be but in part any longer, but become whole and complete." Augustine, *On Man's Perfection in Righteousness*, 13.19. See also *On the Trinity*, 14.17.23.

40. Luther, *Heidelberg*, Thesis 6.

41. "It is His own gifts that God crowns, not your merits—if, at least, your merits are of your own self, not of Him. If, indeed, they are such, they are evil; and God does not crown them; but if they are good, they are God's gifts . . . If, then, your good merits are God's gifts, God does not crown your merits as your merits, but as His own gifts." Augustine, *On Grace and Free Will*, 6.15.

42. "This is clear from Thesis 4. To trust in works, which one ought to do in fear, is equivalent to giving oneself the honor and taking it from God, to whom fear is due in connection with every work. But this is completely wrong, namely to please oneself, to enjoy oneself in one's works, and to adore oneself as an idol. He who is self-confident and without fear of God, however, acts entirely in this manner. For if he had fear he would not be self-confident, and for this reason he would not be pleased with himself, but he would be pleased with God. In the second place, it is clear from the words of the Psalmist (Ps 143:2), 'Enter not into judgment with thy servant,' and Ps 32:5, 'I said: I will confess my transgressions to the Lord' etc. But that these are not venial sins is clear because these passages state that confession and repentance are not necessary for venial sins. If, therefore, they are mortal sins and 'all the saints intercede for them,' as it is stated in the same place, then the works of the saints are mortal sins. But the works of the saints are good works, wherefore they are meritorious for them only through the fear of their humble confession. In the third place, it is clear from the Lord's Prayer, 'Forgive us our trespasses' (Matt 6:12). This is a prayer of the saints, therefore those trespasses are good works for which they pray. But that these are mortal sins is clear from the following verse, 'If you do not forgive men their trespasses, neither will your

> 8. By so much more are the works of man mortal sins when they
> are done without fear and in unadulterated, evil self-security.[43]

Luther is not saying that the believer must live in constant terror of committing "mortal sins" when performing his good works. The German thinker means that our hope and trust must not be in these good works, but in the work of Christ alone. In the Word made flesh, man has confidence, assurance and hope, but if man put his trust in his moral achievements, then his works would actually become "mortal sins" for the reasons that have been mentioned above. Moreover, in proof 8, Luther sets forth a stark contraposition between humility and pride, where humility belongs to those who perform good works not trusting in themselves but in God alone by faith, while pride appertains to those who do good works while trusting in themselves and using these works as a source of "self-security."

Augustine employs a very similar pride-humility dialectic in several places. For example, he teaches that God sometimes withholds his help from the believer in order to protect him from *pride* and teach him *humility*, that is, humble and absolute dependence on God: "In some cases, too, He declines to help even His righteous servants . . . in order that (while in His sight no man living is justified) we may always feel it to be our duty to give Him thanks for mercifully bearing with us, and so, by holy humility, be healed of that first cause of all our failings, even the swellings of pride."[44] For Augustine, this pride was indeed the first sin, the one committed by Adam.[45] In opposition to this, Augustine places the ideal humility and

---

father forgive your trespasses' (Matt 6:15). Note that these trespasses are such that, if unforgiven, they would condemn them, unless they pray this prayer sincerely and forgive others. In the fourth place, it is clear from Rev 21:27, 'Nothing unclean shall enter into it' (the kingdom of heaven). But everything that hinders entrance into the kingdom of heaven is mortal sin (or it would be necessary to interpret the concept of »mortal sin« in another way). Venial sin, however, hinders because it makes the soul unclean and has no place in the kingdom of heaven. Consequently, etc." Luther, *Heidelberg*, Proof 7.

43. "The inevitable deduction from the preceding thesis is clear. For where there is no fear there is no humility. Where there is no humility there is pride, and where there is pride there are the wrath and judgment of God, 'for God opposes the haughty.' Indeed, if pride would cease there would be no sin anywhere." *Ibid.*, Proof 8.

44. Augustine, *On Merit and the Forgiveness of Sins, and the Baptism of Infants*, 3.13.23.

45. "That which he has understood in another sense, is after all most truly said: 'Pride is the commencement of all sin;' because it was this which overthrew the devil, from whom arose the origin of sin; and afterwards, when his malice and envy pursued man, who was yet standing in his uprightness, it subverted him in the same way in which he himself fell. For the serpent, in fact, only sought for the door of pride whereby to enter when he said, 'You shall be as gods' (Gen 3:5) Truly then is it said, 'Pride is the

perfect example of the second Adam, Jesus Christ.[46] Moreover, in contrast to the pride of the "earthly city" (the unbelieving world), Augustine insists that the "city of God" (the church of God) must live according to the example of humility given by the incarnate Logos.[47]

Augustine also explains why these works must be done in pious fear and trembling, and not in security, if they are actually not the works of men themselves but the works of God in them. The answer is, again, because of pride, the most subtle and frequent of all sins: "All other sins only prevail in evil deeds; pride only has to be guarded against in things that are rightly done. Whence it happens that those persons are admonished not to attribute to their own power the gifts of God, nor to plume themselves thereon, lest by so doing they should perish with a heavier perdition than if they had done no good at all."[48] Also in this case, this does not mean that the believer must live in a constant state of fear, but that he should find his security not in himself or in his works, but in the work of Christ crucified alone.[49]

Augustine and Luther appear to be in agreement. Their distinctively Christian philosophy and ethics do not permit them to attribute anything to fallen, sinful man, but rather to attribute everything to God. Christianity often faces the charge of "moralism." This is probably the oddest and most unfounded charge ever made against a genuine Christian philosophy. The message of the cross, on the contrary, reveals exactly that natural man is naturally inclined to moralism, that is, to consider himself good and acceptable to God by his own power and will. Augustine and Luther know who the God of Scripture is and know who man is. This is why any pride or even self-confidence must be totally rejected, and replaced by

---

commencement of all sin' (Sir 10:13); and, *'The beginning of pride is when a man departs from God'* (Sir 10:12)." Augustine, *On Nature and Grace*, 29.33.

46. "Inasmuch as there is nothing more adverse to love than envy, and as pride is the mother of envy, the same Lord Jesus Christ, God-man, is both a manifestation of divine love towards us, and an example of human humility with us, to the end that our great swelling might be cured by a greater counteracting remedy. For here is great misery, proud man! But there is greater mercy, a humble God! Take this love, therefore, as the end that is set before you, to which you are to refer all that you say, and, whatever you narrate, narrate it in such a manner that he to whom you are discoursing on hearing may believe, on believing may hope, on hoping may love." Augustine, *On the Catechising of the Uninstructed*, 4.8.

47. Augustine, *The City of God*, 14.13.

48. Augustine, *On Nature and Grace*, 27.31. See also *On Rebuke and Grace*, 9.24.

49. For other Augustinian passages regarding the humility-pride dialectic, see also *First Epistle of John*, 8.1, 8.9; *The City of God*, 14.13.1; 19.4.1–12.2.

humility and an acknowledgement of one's absolute dependence. Wisdom and morality are by grace alone through faith alone.

> 9. *To say that works without Christ are dead, but not mortal, appears to constitute a perilous surrender of the fear of God.*[50]

> 10. *Indeed, it is very difficult to see how a work can be dead and at the same time not a harmful and mortal sin.*[51]

These theses constitute an answer to the sophism that some works can be dead without being mortal or deadly, a sophism that Luther denies and confutes using the primary source of his theology, Holy Scripture. By this, Luther is probably referring to an objection that the dead works of a man without faith do not necessarily make him a spiritually dead rational being. Luther, however, believes that the definition of "dead" and "mortal" must be taken or inferred from the Bible, and not derived from such an arbitrary, and in this case fictitious, grammatical distinction. This is why he does not devote much time to it, since it is refuted by the logical implication of what both Luther himself has already said with Augustine's support, who, in fact, also claims that mankind is "dead both in soul and body: in soul, because of sin; in body, because of the punishment of sin, and through this also in body because of sin,"[52] as we have seen in chapter 1. Moreover, Scripture is the source of the theology and philosophy of these authors, and Luther points out that Scripture does not make this particular distinction.

50. "For in this way men become certain and therefore haughty, which is perilous. For in such a way God is constantly deprived of the glory which is due him and which is transferred to other things, since one should strive with all diligence to give him the glory—the sooner the better. For this reason the Bible advises us, 'Do not delay being converted to the Lord.' For if that person offends him who withdraws glory from him, how much more does that person offend him who continues to withdraw glory from him and does this boldly! But whoever is not in Christ or who withdraws from him withdraws glory from him, as is well known." Luther, *Heidelberg*, Proof 9.

51. "This I prove in the following way: Scripture does not speak of dead things in such a manner, stating that something is not mortal which is nevertheless dead. Indeed, neither does grammar, which says that 'dead' is a stronger term than 'mortal.' For the grammarians call a mortal work one which kills, a 'dead' work not one that has been killed, but one that is not alive. But God despises what is not alive, as is written in Prov 15:8, 'The sacrifice of the wicked is an abomination to the Lord.' Second, the will must do something with respect to such a dead work, namely, either love or hate it. The will cannot hate a dead work since the will is evil. Consequently the will loves a dead work, and therefore it loves something dead. In that act itself it thus induces an evil work of the will against God whom it should love and honor in this and in every deed." *Ibid.*, Proof 10.

52. Augustine, *On the Trinity*, 4.3.5.

*11. Arrogance cannot be avoided or true hope be present unless
the judgment of condemnation is feared in every work.*[53]

*12. In the sight of God sins are then truly venial when they are
feared by men to be mortal.*[54]

With theses 11 and 12, Luther intends to give the *coup de grâce* to man's
fabricated good works and morality, and to the misleading hope that man
places in them. In light of the preceding theses, theses 11 and 12 state the
absolute invalidity of every work of man when man performs such works
believing that in so doing he can satisfy or please God by their mere external performance. Instead, "condemnation" must indeed be feared because
"there is no person who has this pure hope, as we said above, and since we
still place some confidence in the creature, it is clear that we must, because
of impurity in all things, fear the judgment of God."[55] We have already
seen these concepts in thesis 4, and it can be argued that theses 11 and 12
are introduced to summarize and strengthen what has already been said.

As we have seen, in our discussion of the will and conversion, man's
absolute dependence on God for righteousness and moral improvement
does not make man a passive puppet maneuvered by a divine mechanism.
Will, motivations, and desires are involved in the divine work that has
been discussed in this and previous chapters. Nevertheless, it is important to remember the anthropological basis for the assertion of Augustine
and Luther, who both consider man according to his fallenness, because
of which man's will, motivations, and desires have been subverted from
being God-centered to man-centered.[56] Man, however, is not the highest

53. "This is clear from Thesis 4. For it is impossible to trust in God unless one has
despaired in all creatures and knows that nothing can profit one without God. Since
there is no person who has this pure hope, as we said above, and since we still place
some confidence in the creature, it is clear that we must, because of impurity in all
things, fear the judgment of God. Thus arrogance must be avoided, not only in the
work, but in the inclination also, that is, it must displease us still to have confidence in
the creature." Luther, *Heidelberg*, Proof 11.

54. "This becomes sufficiently clear from what has been said. For as much as we accuse ourselves, so much God pardons us, according to the verse, 'Confess your misdeed
so that you will be justified' (cf. Isa 43:26), and according to another (Ps 141:4), 'Incline
not my heart to any evil, to busy myself with wicked deeds.'" *Ibid.*, Proof 12.

55. *Ibid.*, Proof 11.

56. "The devil, then, would not have ensnared man in the open and manifest sin
of doing what God had forbidden, had man not already begun to live for himself. It
was this that made him listen with pleasure to the words, You shall be as gods, Gen 3:5
which they would much more readily have accomplished by obediently adhering to
their supreme and true end than by proudly living to themselves. For created gods are
gods not by virtue of what is in themselves, but by a participation of the true God. By

good. God is. Therefore, since man is turned and curved upon himself, and since he is ethically inclined to evil because of the fall, truly spiritual autonomous will and moral progress in true holiness are impossible because man is entirely dedicated to something that was created good but that now is spiritually corrupt, that is, to himself. This is the reason why we have seen that Augustine extends the absolute necessity of Christ not only to the regeneration of the will into freedom and conversion to God and the performing of good, but also to all the subsequent moments and every virtuous effort of the life of the enlightened and regenerated man, including also the restoration unto righteousness of motivations and desires. This progress in virtue will always be incomplete in this earthly life, for its full completion is the eschatological principle which the renewed man must continually bear in mind throughout his intellectual and experiential pilgrimage.

> Himself [Jesus Christ] being both Priest and Sacrifice, He might bring about the remission of sins, that is to say, might bring it about through the Mediator between God and men, the man Christ Jesus, by whom we are reconciled to God, the cleansing from sin being accomplished. For men are separated from God only by sins, from which we are in this life cleansed not by our own virtue, but by the divine compassion; through His indulgence, not through our own power. For, *whatever virtue we call our own is itself bestowed upon us by His goodness.* And we might attribute too much to ourselves while in the flesh, unless we lived in the receipt of pardon until we laid it down. This is the reason why there has been vouchsafed to us, through the Mediator, this grace, that we who are polluted by sinful flesh should be cleansed by the likeness of sinful flesh. By this grace of God, wherein He has shown His great compassion toward us, we are both governed by faith in this life, and, after this life, are led onwards to the fullest perfection by the vision of immutable truth.[57]

Also here must be borne in mind the background of man's spiritual death that results in the impossibility of any autonomous moral progress in

---

craving to be more, man becomes less; and by aspiring to be self-sufficing, he fell away from Him who truly suffices him. Accordingly, this wicked desire which prompts man to please himself as if he were himself light, and which thus turns him away from that light by which, had he followed it, he would himself have become light." Augustine, *The City of God*, 14.5. See also the entire section 1–9 of book 14 for a wider discussion of the subject.

57. *Ibid.*, 10.22. Emphasis added.

righteousness according to God's standard. The standard of God is His revealed holy law, which God demands man keeps perfectly, not only externally with man's outward deeds, but also inwardly with man's desires, motivations and thoughts. This law is good and holy in itself but, according to Luther "fallen man misuses the best things in the worst manner."[58] God's law is "the most salutary doctrine of life,"[59] but man is naturally and immediately prone to ascribe to himself the ability to honor and fulfill this law as God commands, namely, perfectly. Good works are equally commendable; the problem arises when man puts his trust in them, making good works and the moral law the means for gaining God's approval or even worse, an end in itself. The law of God is good and good works are lawful and required, but man, on hearing this, misuses his own will, and misunderstands his own ethical nature so that he considers himself able to perform these works, which, he thinks, will make him righteous and, therefore, worthy of God's grace. Man always misuses everything he uses, placing in them that trust which must be placed in the Creator. This is one of the other reasons why a supernatural saving enlightenment is necessary. Man needs an internal operation that may correct his ethics which, as we have said, is upside down.[60] This supernatural work is necessary to give to man the right epistemology to know himself and everything else. This is the only solution and, as Augustine says, "through this love of the Creator everyone uses even creatures well. Without this love of the Creator no one uses any creature well."[61]

We have now explained the ethical constitution of fallen man. Moreover, we understand his relation to the law of God and to God himself. We know that true righteousness is unattainable through mere human efforts. Most importantly, we have seen that Augustine and Luther are largely in agreement on this issue. According to both of them, man must

---

58. Luther, *Heidelberg*, Thesis 24.

59. *Ibid.*, Thesis 1.

60. "From yourself you have the ill doing, from God you have the well doing. On the other hand, see perverse men, how preposterous they are. What they do well, they will needs ascribe to themselves; if they do ill, they will needs accuse God. Reverse this distorted and preposterous proceeding, which puts the thing, as one may say, head downwards, which makes that undermost which is uppermost, and that upwards which is downwards. Do you want to make God undermost and yourself uppermost? You go headlong, not elevatest yourself; for He is always above. What then? You well, and God ill? Nay rather, say this, if you would speak more truly, I ill, He well; and what I do well from Him is the well-doing: for from myself whatever I do is ill." Augustine, *First Epistle of John* 8.2.

61. Augustine, *Against Julian*, 4.3.33.

utterly "despair" of himself, because any philosophical theorization which seeks autonomous morality is, in the eyes of God, nothing but hypocrisy and self-exaltation. However, the despair of the individual is not an end in itself, but is compensated by the possibility of true righteousness. We must now investigate *how* man can obtain true righteousness, or more accurately, how he can *receive* this righteousness.

CHAPTER 4

THE RIGHTEOUSNESS OF GOD

THESES 25–28 CONSTITUTE THE third section of the *Heidelberg Disputation*. They give the solution to the two problems which, according to Luther, afflict mankind: the bondage of man's will and his consequent inability to keep the law of God. It should be clear that this chapter is strictly related to the previous one, inasmuch as here the German thinker develops further man's ethical powerlessness to perform good deeds and to show moral virtues from God's point of view. Luther's remedy is faith, a remedy which is diametrically opposed to any secular moral philosophy and is usually considered by secular philosophers to be intellectual suicide. In relation to this, Luther criticises Aristotle in theses 25 and 28. His interest is mainly, but not exclusively, Aristotle's ethics. It may be contended that Luther sees Aristotelian ethics as a philosophical version of Pelagian theology. To express this more precisely, for the German theologian, Pelagianism, with the Scholasticism which he opposed and which he considered to be Pelagian in nature, has its philosophical and theological source in Aristotle rather than in Scripture.

In relation to this last assertion, chapter 6 will seek to demonstrate that any ethics set forth independently of a consistent understanding of Christianity is basically constructed on an Aristotelian or Pelagian foundation. This is not to confuse Aristotelian ethics with Pelagian theology. Nor does it mean that these philosophies are *purposely* and *consciously* built on such principles. The point is that the two share a common approach to morality. Christian philosophy is so unique and radical that it is naturally antithetical to any philosophy developed from first principles which are not Christian axioms; similarly, any philosophy developed from principles other than Christian principles naturally conflicts with Christian philosophy. Christian philosophy in general, and the philosophy of Augustine and Luther in particular, the subject of our study, develops entirely on the presupposition of man's *absolute* dependence on God. In antithesis to this, secular philosophy always attributes something to man, and such secular philosophies consider man, at least in some respects, *independent* of God.

The character of the philosophy of Luther and Augustine places them in diametrical opposition to much of the philosophy of the centuries which preceded and followed them. In the closing chapter of the present book, I will discuss the Aristotelian or Pelagian ground of this auto-soteriological philosophical approach, or what Luther would call the "theology of glory." It is impossible to discuss in detail every single philosophy or philosopher of these historical periods. Therefore, as the *Heidelberg Disputation* has been chosen as representative of Luther's thought; in the same way, Aristotelian ethics, the Kantian philosophy of religion, and Leibniz's theodicy will be adopted as representatives of the philosophy opposed by the Augustinian Luther. For the moment, however, we must focus on the Augustinian nature of Luther's treatment of righteousness obtained by grace alone through faith alone.

> 25. *He is not righteous who does much, but he who, without work, believes much in Christ.*[1]

As we already began to see in the previous chapter, man is naturally inclined to think that he may be or become righteous by living according to and maintaining a certain standard of morality, which consists in

---

1. "For the righteousness of God is not acquired by means of acts frequently repeated, as Aristotle taught, but it is imparted by faith, for 'He who through faith is righteous shall live' (Rom 1:17), and 'Man believes with his heart and so is justified' (Rom 10:10). Therefore I wish to have the words 'without work' understood in the following manner: Not that the righteous person does nothing, but that his works do not make him righteous, rather that his righteousness creates works. For grace and faith are infused without our works. After they have been imparted the works follow. Thus Rom. 3:20 states, 'No human being will be justified in His sight by works of the law,' and, 'For we hold that man is justified by faith apart from works of law' (Rom 3:28). In other words, works contribute nothing to justification. Therefore man knows that works which he does by such faith are not his but God's. For this reason he does not seek to become justified or glorified through them, but seeks God. His justification by faith in Christ is sufficient to him. Christ is his wisdom, righteousness, etc., as 1 Cor 1:30 has it, that he himself may be Christ's vessel and instrument (*operatio seu instrumentum*)." Luther, *Heidelberg*, Proof 25.

accomplishing certain works, which are considered good, and of abstaining from other works, which are considered evil. Luther, however, turns the starting point of this ethical concept upside down. In fact, for him man's works do not produce righteousness, but righteousness creates works. The cause is that man is not righteous, but sinful and incurably selfish. Therefore, man's only hope is in a righteousness which comes from outside of himself, the righteousness of God, which is obtained by "grace and faith"[2] which "are infused without our works."[3] This does not mean "that the righteous person does nothing"[4] but rather that true righteousness is the basis of good works, and not, as Aristotle teaches, that good repeated virtuous works make a man righteous or virtuous.

Also this thesis, as well as the entire section, is set forth according to Augustinian presuppositions. Luther shows his agreement with Augustine in that man's hope for righteousness and morality is found only in God's transforming grace and in faith in him, after the acknowledgment of his own sinfulness (an acknowledgment which itself also is a gift from God). Only after grace is bestowed and faith is given is man empowered to perform good works. To be more specific, it is better to allow Augustine to define what he means by "grace" and "faith": "the grace of God through Jesus Christ our Lord must be apprehended—as that by which alone men are delivered from evil, and without which they do absolutely no good thing, whether in thought, or will and affection, or in action; not only in order that they may know, by the manifestation of that grace, what should be done, but moreover in order that, by its enabling [power], they may do with love what they know [ought to be done]."[5] Augustine defines faith also as a gift of God; the beginning of conversion and the act of believing in God are also mere gifts from God: "even faith itself cannot be had without God's mercy, and that it is the gift of God."[6]

It is not a misrepresentation to claim that the adversaries of Augustine (Pelagius and the Semi-Pelagians) held to a doctrine of Aristotelian ethics expressed in Christian theological terminology. Pelagian and Semi-Pelagian positions have already been summarized.[7] Augustine, on the other

2. *Ivi.*

3. *Ivi.*

4. *Ivi.*

5. Augustine, *On Rebuke and Grace*, 3. For more Augustinian definitions of "grace," see also *The Gospel of John*, 17.6; *Against Two Letters of the Pelagians*, 4.11.

6. Augustine, *On Grace and Free Will*, 7.17.

7. See chapter 2, footnote 2 and 3. See also chapter 6, footnote 2.

hand, believed that true righteousness is the basis of a true moral life, and not the other way around. Commenting on Romans 1:14–17, Augustine asserts that the righteousness mentioned by Paul is ". . . the righteousness of God . . . it is called the righteousness of God, because by His bestowal of it He makes us righteous, just as we read that *salvation is the Lord's*, because He makes us safe . . . By this faith of Jesus Christ—that is, the faith which Christ has given to us—we believe it is from God that we now have, and shall have more and more, the ability of living righteously."[8] We thus see that Augustine, as well as Luther, believes that righteousness is the source of moral deeds, and that one does not become righteous by repeated moral acts.

It is true that Augustine usually speaks of "making righteous" instead of "declaring righteous," while Luther would definitely prefer the latter expression. We have seen that "to *declare* a man righteous" is that legal act of God by which he justifies a man in His sight, while "to *make* a man righteous" is that continual and gradual work of God by which God sanctifies or makes his elect holy. For Luther, to say that in justification God "makes the believer righteous" would be to mix the two inseparable but still distinguishable elements of God's work. It is true that, according to both Augustine and Luther, sanctification always follows true righteousness. However, Augustine did not develop this important distinction between "declaring" righteous and "making" righteous. In this case, it must be granted that the perspective of Augustine is somewhat different from that of Luther.

Nevertheless, it is also true that Augustine offered a legal interpretation of the biblical passage, which is the interpretation that Luther prefers, although he did not develop his insight. In the work of justification, God, in freely giving to the believer his righteousness, does not materially 'infuse' this righteousness into the believer. Rather, he, as the highest and only Lawgiver, merely *declares* or *reckons* the believer righteous from a legal point of view. We can read this insight of Augustine in *The Spirit and the Letter*: "Or else the term '*They shall be justified*' is used in the sense of, They shall be deemed, or reckoned as just, as it is predicated of a certain man in the Gospel, '*But he, willing to justify himself,*' (Luke 10:29)—meaning that he wished to be thought and accounted just. In like manner, we attach one meaning to the statement, '*God sanctifies His saints,*' and another to the words, '*Sanctified be Your name*' (Matt 6:9) for in the former case we suppose the words to mean that He makes those to be saints who

---

8. Augustine, *The Spirit and the Letter*, 11.18.

were not saints before, and in the latter, that the prayer would have that which is always holy in itself be also regarded as holy by men—in a word, be feared with a hallowed awe."[9] For some reason, the English translation of this passage omits the Latin adverb *certe*, which means "certainly" or "doubtlessly."[10] Thus it would be more accurate to translate it something like the following: "The term '*They shall be justified*' can certainly also have the sense of, They shall be deemed, or reckoned as just."

Augustine evaluated as at least a plausible interpretation the one that Luther holds as the only correct one and that Luther categorized as follows: "If this doctrine [of justification by faith alone] be lost, then is also the doctrine of truth life, and salvation, also lost and gone."[11] Augustine, however, did not develop this interpretative insight. Luther, with the Reformers, felt the need to develop Augustine's idea. Nevertheless, the fact that Augustine was somehow restricted in the development of this particular point does not disprove the fact that the African theologian believed that salvation in general and justification in particular are accomplished by God alone, by his grace alone and through faith alone. Thus, it also does not disprove the fact that Augustine places righteousness before good works, i.e., as the necessary basis of good works. On the contrary, the legal interpretation already envisioned by Augustine himself seems to fit more consistently with the theology of absolute grace advocated by the same Augustine.

Returning to the thesis, Luther claimed that the righteous man "knows that works which he does by such faith are not his but God's."[12] This does not imply that "the righteous person does nothing."[13] In fact, only the believer believes and performs good works. But the believer knows that it is God who is the source of his faith and good works, or, to use Luther's words, the righteous man knows that the "works he does by such faith are not his but God's." Augustine expresses the same idea in several places, where he also does not deny that man actually does something. Nevertheless, this work is to be attributed to God alone: "It is certain that we keep the commandments if we will; but because the will is prepared by the Lord, we must ask of Him for such a force of will as suffices to make us act by the willing. It is certain that it is we that *will* when we will, but it

---

9. *Ibid.*, 26.45.

10. A famous Italian translation does not omit the word in question: "La frase: *Saranno giustificati*, può certo [certe] avere anche questo significato: 'Saranno ritenuti giusti', 'saranno reputati giusti.'" Agostino, *Lo Spirito e la Lettera*, 26.45.

11. Luther, *Commentary on Galatians*, xi.

12. Luther, *Heidelberg*, Proof 25.

13. *Ivi.*

is He who makes us will what is good, . . . It is certain that it is we that act when we act; but it is He who makes us act, by applying efficacious powers to our will."[14] According to the African thinker, this implies that when God seems to crown our virtues and good works, what he is actually doing is crowning his own gifts.[15]

Augustine indeed believed that works contribute nothing to justification, that is, to the receiving of God's righteousness for salvation through the means of conversion and repentance. In fact, if good works flow only from that righteousness that is freely and graciously given by God, it is implied that, before man receives this righteousness, his good works do not have any positive role. In the work of salvation, God uses proper means, both subjective and internal means, such as faith and conversion, and external and objective means, such as the preaching and sacraments.[16] However, this faith is a gift of God, and without this faith good works have no ground. In fact, even the act of believing, that is, faith itself, is the gift of God that he bestows only on those whom he has eternally predestined before the foundation of the world.[17] Therefore, here also Luther's defense of the Augustinian nature of his theses is well grounded. Along the same line of thought of the German thinker, this is what Augustine says: "Works proceed from faith, and not faith from works. Therefore it is from Him that we have works of righteousness, from whom comes also faith itself."[18] In the economy of both salvation and revelation, Augustine, like Luther, gives temporal priority to faith in Christ for the obtaining of righteousness.

> 26. The law says, "do this," and it is never done. Grace says, "believe in this," and everything is already done.[19]

14. Augustine, *On Grace and Free Will*, 16.32.

15. "It is His own gifts that God crowns, not your merits—if, at least, your merits are of your own self, not of Him. If, indeed, they are such, they are evil; and God does not crown them; but if they are good, they are God's gifts . . . If, then, your good merits are God's gifts, God does not crown your merits as your merits, but as His own gifts." *Ibid.*, 6.15.

16. Augustine, *On Rebuke and Grace*, 15:46–47, 16.49; *On the Gift of Perseverance*, 14.34.

17. Augustine, *On the Predestination of the Saints*, 17.34.

18. *Ibid.*, 7.17.

19. "The first part is clear from what has been stated by the Apostle and his interpreter, St. Augustine, in many places. And it has been stated often enough above that the 'law' 'works wrath' and keeps all men under the curse. The second part is clear from the same sources, for faith justifies. And the law (says St. Augustine) commands what faith obtains. For through faith Christ is in us, indeed, one with us. Christ is just and has fulfilled all the commands of God, wherefore we also fulfill everything through him

In the proof of this thesis, Luther mentions the apostle Paul and Augustine. Luther claims that the law and its mere external accomplishment of the law obtain for man neither righteousness nor salvation. Rather, the requirements of the law, what the law commands, can be obtained only through faith in Christ. This flows from Christian theology, according to which Christ, being true God and true man, perfectly kept all the commandments of God's law with a perfect love for God. Only when Christ becomes "ours" are true righteousness and salvation obtained. Faith, being the means by which God spiritually unites the believer to Christ, is therefore the only way of righteousness and salvation and that righteousness is the only thing that satisfies God's law. Accordingly, Luther says that when the law commands, nothing is done; on the contrary, when grace commands faith, the law itself is entirely satisfied. The point of the law is to direct the believer to God's grace. Luther claims that Augustine is in agreement with him, but he does not give any specific reference. However, it is not difficult to see that Luther's claim is accurate, in light of what I have already said regarding the topics of law, grace and faith.

Paraphrasing, we can say that thesis 27 recalls the very well known Augustinian expression, "Give what thou commandest and command what thou wilt."[20] Luther could not have failed to recall Augustine's famous motto, which played an essential role in the Pelagian controversy. However, the wording of the thesis and proof ("the law [says St. Augustine] commands what faith obtains"[21]) bears resemblance to another Augustinian passage in *The Spirit and the Letter*. This passage once again demonstrates the distinctive Augustinianism at the heart of the *Heidelberg Disputation* and of Luther's whole teaching, since these theses give a brief summary of his entire system and the thought of the Reformation. For Augustine, man's attempts to observe the law achieve basically nothing of what the law requires: "What the law of works enjoins by menace, that the law of faith secures by faith."[22] "Secures" is the translation of *impetrate*, from *impetro*, which means to achieve, bring to pass, get, obtain, procure, and so on. Augustine goes on to give a version of his motto which was mentioned above: "by the law of works, God says to us, Do what I command you; but by the law of faith we say to God, Give me what You command."[23] Righteousness

---

since he was made ours through faith." Luther, *Heidelberg*, Proof 26.

20. Augustine, *Confessions*, 10.29.40–31.45.

21. Luther, *Heidelberg*, Proof 26.

22. Augustine, *The Spirit and the Letter*, 13.22.

23. *Ivi.*

and salvation are achieved only through faith, because faith legally and spiritually unites the believer to Christ. And Christ is the only one who has perfectly fulfilled the law with perfect love, as God demands. Therefore, because the believer is *in* Christ, the legal condition of the believer is not what he is in himself (a sinner) but what Christ is (a perfectly righteous man).

Moreover, also Augustine held that "the 'law' 'works wrath' and keeps all men under the curse."[24] The expression 'the law works wrath' is a quotation from Rom 4:15. The argument is simple. Since man's free will is enslaved to sin, the law of God cannot help him to be saved and righteous. The only thing the law can do is to tell man what he must do and what he must not do. Moreover, the law points to faith and grace in Christ. Thus, the law without grace only brings wrath and the curse, because it tells man what he should do but what he is neither able nor willing to do, as well as the things which he should not do but which he is inclined and willing to do. As Augustine says, "the Lord Himself not only shows us what evil we should shun, and what good we should do, which is all that the letter of the law is able to effect; but He moreover helps us that we may shun evil and do good, which none can do without the Spirit of grace; and if this be wanting, the law comes in merely to make us guilty and to slay us."[25] We have to remember that Augustine firmly believed that the law of God is good and honorable. But this law has no power in itself to give righteousness and salvation: "We do not then make void the law through faith, but we establish the law (Rom 3:31) which by terrifying leads to faith. Thus certainly the law works wrath, that the mercy of God may bestow grace on the sinner, frightened and turned to the fulfilment of the righteousness of the law through Jesus Christ our Lord."[26] Not that the law is left unfulfilled. On the contrary, it has been perfectly fulfilled. But, as we have seen, mere man cannot fulfill the law. Only the one who is true God and true man can, that is, Christ. In fact, the believer has fulfilled the law, not in himself, but *in Christ*, to whom he is united by faith. Thus, Augustine praises the Apostle Paul who "casts away those past attainments of his righteousness, as '*losses*' and '*dung*' that he may '*win Christ and be found in Him, not having his own righteousness, which is of the law*.'"[27]

---

24. Luther, *Heidelberg*, Proof 19.
25. Augustine, *On Correction and Grace*, 1.2.
26. Augustine, *Against Two Letters of the Pelagians*, 4.11.5.
27. *Ibid.*, 7.20.

27. Actually one should call the work of Christ an acting work (operans) and our work an accomplished work (operatum), and thus an accomplished work pleasing to God by the grace of the acting work.[28]

This thesis does not add much to what Luther has already said. It merely repeats that Christ works in our good works. However, it is interesting to note the "sacramental language of medieval theology"[29] that Luther uses. It seems to recall the Augustinian description of Christ as our sacrament and example.[30] It means that Christ must first be ours by faith. After that, the "attractive" work of Christ in the believer arouses in the believer good works which are performed after the perfect example of Christ. Nevertheless, the prior work of grace in us is absolutely necessary. Also here, we cite Augustine: "grace, not due, but free, precedes, that by it good works may be done; but if good works should precede, grace should be repaid, as it were, to works, and thus grace should be no more grace."[31]

28. The love of God does not find, but creates, that which is pleasing to it. The love of man comes into being through that which is pleasing to it.[32]

28. "Since Christ lives in us through faith so he arouses us to do good works through that living faith in his work, for the works which he does are the fulfilment of the commands of God given us through faith. If we look at them we are moved to imitate them. For this reason the Apostle says, 'Therefore be imitators of God, as beloved children' (Eph 5:1). Thus deeds of mercy are aroused by the works through which he has saved us, as St. Gregory says: 'Every act of Christ is instruction for us, indeed, a stimulant.' If his action is in us it lives through faith, for it is exceedingly attractive according to the verse, 'Draw me after you, let us make haste' (Song 1:4) toward the fragrance 'of your anointing oils' (Song 1:3), that is, 'your works.'" Luther, *Heidelberg*, Proof 27.

29. Forde, *On being a Theologian of the Cross*, 112.

30. Augustine, *On the Trinity*, 4.3.6; 4.7.11; 4.13.17.

31. Augustine, *Against Two Letters of the Pelagians*, 2.7.15.

32. "The second part is clear and is accepted by all philosophers and theologians, for the object of love is its cause, assuming, according to Aristotle, that all power of the soul is passive and material and active only in receiving something. Thus it is also demonstrated that Aristotle's philosophy is contrary to theology since in all things it seeks those things which are its own and receives rather than gives something good. The first part is clear because the love of God which lives in man loves sinners, evil persons, fools, and weaklings in order to make them righteous, good, wise, and strong. Rather than seeking its own good, the love of God flows forth and bestows good. Therefore sinners are 'attractive' because they are loved; they are not loved because they are 'attractive': For this reason the love of man avoids sinners and evil persons. Thus Christ says: 'For I came not to call the righteous, but sinners' (Matt 9:13). This is the love of the cross, born of the cross, which turns in the direction where it does not find good which it may enjoy, but where it may confer good upon the bad and needy person. 'It is

From the perspective of the Augustinian philosophy of the cross, any moral philosophy that includes a theory of the divine in its development, if not properly and consistently derived from Biblical teaching, consists basically of this: man, by virtue of his working, makes himself worthy to be saved and to be considered with favor by God. This means that, according to these philosophies, God looks for what pleases him in the being and in the works of man. Accordingly, God bestows his favor or disfavor according to whether he finds in man what, according to this philosophy, supposedly pleases him. This approach is not only evident in the more religious Pelagian theology, but also in more philosophical systems, such as, for example, the philosophy of religion of Immanuel Kant. According to Augustine and Luther, Pelagianism is the natural religion which is the fruit of man's intellectual attempt to develop a religion based on his mere reason, apart from revelation. Here, by 'natural' is not intended 'most proper' or 'true', but merely more spontaneous and in accordance with the ethical constitution and ethical presuppositions of man considered in himself.

Luther, through Augustine, overturns all this, for, according to him, God does not look for what pleases him in man. Rather, he creates in man what pleases him. Thus, Luther believes that God creates this love in man *from nothing*, that is, without any cooperation from man and independently of man's worthiness or unworthiness. This means that, in opposition to Aristotelian ethics and Kantian religion, a man is "attractive" (in God's eyes) *because* he is loved (by God), and not the other way around. In brief: man is accepted by God because God loved man first, and not because man loves God. To love God first would be impossible. In fact, we have already seen that natural man does not love God at all. On the contrary, he hates God. Rather, God bestows his love upon a sinful and depraved man so that man may love the one who is holy and righteous. We may find a similar treatment of love in the philosophy of Augustine.

This is the final thesis of the *Heidelberg Disputation*. I do not think that it is fortuitous that the closing thesis of Luther's disputation includes a discussion of love. As is well known, love is an essential issue in Augustine's thinking. For the African theologian, all our inner and outward activities, both intellectual and practical, must be led by love toward God,

---

more blessed to give than to receive' (Acts 20:35), says the Apostle. Hence Ps 41:1 states, 'Blessed is he who considers the poor,' for the intellect cannot by nature comprehend an object which does not exist, that is the poor and needy person, but only a thing which does exist, that is the true and good. Therefore it judges according to appearances, is a respecter of persons, and judges according to that which can be seen, etc." Luther, *Heidelberg*, Proof 28.

first of all, and secondly by love toward our neighbor.[33] This love cannot be any love whatsoever, but the ordered love inspired and shaped by God's truth.[34] In relation to the Augustinian nature of the *Heidelberg Disputation*, we must determine if Augustine holds the same idea which is both the foundation and the conclusion of Luther's position: man is by nature unable and unwilling to love God, unless God himself first bestows his regenerative love.

We can read that for Augustine love for heavenly things is impossible unless it is first given by God. The resolution of love is in itself a good thing, and every good thing comes from the greatest good, namely God himself. However, it must be remembered that man's fallen state twists every activity of mankind, love included. In fact, it is not the case that man does not love at all by himself, but in this case his love is always self-love or love for other creatures or things rather than for the Creator.[35] Conversely, true love is always first directed toward God. However, man is sinful and delights in wickedness and also when he seems to be loving, he does not love through God. This means that the beginning of such true love must also be created by God.[36]

Augustine often identifies love with the Holy Spirit, who supernaturally works true love in man's heart: "Love, therefore, which is of God and is God, is especially the Holy Spirit, by whom the love of God is shed abroad

33. Augustine, *On Christian Doctrine*, 1.26.27; 1.35.39–40.44.

34. Augustine, *On Christian Doctrine*, 1.27.28.

35. One eminent example is the famous description of the two cities, the earthly and the heavenly: "Accordingly, two cities have been formed by two loves: the earthly by the love of self, even to the contempt of God; the heavenly by the love of God, even to the contempt of self. The former, in a word, glories in itself, the latter in the Lord. For the one seeks glory from men; but the greatest glory of the other is God, the witness of conscience. The one lifts up its head in its own glory; the other says to its God, '*You are my glory, and the lifter up of mine head.*'" Augustine, *The City of God*, 14.28. See also *Ibid.*, 14.13.1; *Expositions on the Psalms*, 64.2; *The Literal Interpretation of Genesis*, 11.15.20.

36. "Wherefore God does many good things in man which man does not do; but man does none which God does not cause man to do. Accordingly, there would be no desire of good in man from the Lord if it were not a good; but if it is a good, we have it not save from Him who is supremely and incommunicably good . . . Nor is its beginning of ourselves, and its perfection of God; but if love is of God, we have the whole of it from God. May God by all means turn away this folly of making ourselves first in His gifts, Himself last—because His mercy shall prevent me . . . Therefore the blessing of sweetness is God's grace, by which is caused in us that what He prescribes to us delights us, and we desire it—that is, we love it; in which if God does not precede us, not only is it not perfected, but it is not even begun, from us." Augustine, *Against Two Letters of the Pelagians*, 2.9.21. See also *Expositions on the Psalms*, 118.17.2.

in our hearts, by which love the whole Trinity dwells in us."[37] Moreover and more fundamentally, the Holy Spirit is the love that the three persons of the Trinity share, and that consequently is shared between the Trinity and the believing man.[38] The Holy Spirit is the pure and uncreated divine love: "The Holy Spirit is specially called by the name of Love."[39] Therefore, he is the only one who is able to create and restore man to his original condition of love toward God[40] and, consequently, toward the neighbor.[41] All these Augustinian assertions mean that the duo love-Holy Spirit is of central importance also when it comes to the topics of redemption and enlightenment, including the four fundamental subjects that Luther discusses in his *Heidelberg Disputation*.

As Luther placed his view of God-created love in opposition to any doctrine of autonomous self-produced love for God, in a similar way Augustine places his conception of God-created love in opposition to his Pelagian adversaries, who claimed that, while the knowledge of the law of God comes from God, the love for this law and for God arises from man himself. According to Augustine, to say that true love comes from

37. Augustine, *On the Trinity*, 15.18.32.

38. *Ibid.*, 15.19.36–37.

39. *Ibid.*, 15.17.31.

40. "We, however, on our side affirm that the human will is so divinely aided in the pursuit of righteousness, that (in addition to man's being created with a free-will, and in addition to the teaching by which he is instructed how he ought to live) he receives the Holy Ghost, by whom there is formed in his mind a delight in, and a love of, that supreme and unchangeable good which is God, even now while he is still '*walking by faith*' and not yet '*by sight*' (2 Cor 5:7) in order that by this gift to him of the earnest, as it were, of the free gift, he may conceive an ardent desire to cleave to his Maker, and may burn to enter upon the participation in that true light, that it may go well with him from Him to whom he owes his existence. A man's free-will, indeed, avails for nothing except to sin, if he knows not the way of truth; and even after his duty and his proper aim shall begin to become known to him, unless he also take delight in and feel a love for it, he neither does his duty, nor sets about it, nor lives rightly. Now, in order that such a course may engage our affections, God's '*love is shed abroad in our hearts*,' not through the free-will which arises from ourselves, but '*through the Holy Ghost, which is given to us*' (Rom 5:5)'. Augustine, *The Spirit and the Letter*, 3.5.

41. "To proceed to what remains. It may be thought that there is nothing here about man himself, the lover. But to think this, shows a want of clear perception. For it is impossible for one who loves God not to love himself. For he alone has a proper love for himself who aims diligently at the attainment of the chief and true good; and if this is nothing else but God, as has been shown, what is to prevent one who loves God from loving himself? And then, among men should there be no bond of mutual love? Yea, verily; so that we can think of no surer step towards the love of God than the love of man to man." Augustine, *On the Morals of the Catholic Church*, 1.26.48. See also *On Christian Doctrine*, 1.22.21.

us is equivalent to saying that God himself comes from us, because God himself "is love" (1 John 4:6). "In the Pelagian writings," however, "the darkness says, 'Love comes to us of our own selves.'"[42] We have seen that the law and the knowledge of the law are, in themselves, good. Nevertheless, since man is ethically fallen, the African theologian concludes that "the knowledge of the law" does not generate love, but rather "makes a proud transgressor."[43] Accordingly, to say that God gives the knowledge of the law without the necessary love of that law is to say that God poses the problem without giving the solution. For Augustine, this is an inconsistency that would make saving enlightenment pointless and absurd: "Now what can be more absurd, nay, what more insane and more alien from the very sacredness of love itself, than to maintain that from God proceeds the knowledge which, apart from love, puffs us up, while the love which prevents the possibility of this inflation of knowledge springs from ourselves? . . . The true faith, however, and sound doctrine declare that both graces [the knowledge of the law and the love for the law] are from God."[44]

This is because, prior to his enlightenment, man has nothing spiritually good of himself.[45] He is good as a creation of God, but considered morally his free will is bound to sin and his soul is corrupted by it. To expect true love from such a being is impossible: "And should he [Pelagius] consent that we receive love from the grace of God, he must not suppose that any merits of our own preceded our reception of the gift. For what merits could we possibly have had at the time when we loved not God? In order, indeed, that we might receive that love whereby we might love, we were loved while as yet we had no love ourselves . . . we could not have wherewithal to love Him, unless we received it from Him in His first loving us."[46]

For Augustine, as for Luther, the restoration of ordered love in mankind is a prerogative that only the supernatural work of God through the Holy Spirit can have. This has far-reaching implications not only from a theoretical point of view, but also from an ethical perspective. In fact, Augustine even overlaps the meanings of virtue and love, or, at least, shows a very strict relationship between the two elements: "it seems to me that it

---

42. Augustine, *On Grace and Free Will*, 19.40.

43. Augustine, *Against Two Letters of the Pelagians*, 4.5.11.

44. Augustine, *On Grace and Free Will*, 19.40.

45. *Ibid.*, 18.37.

46. Augustine, *On the Grace of Christ and on Original Sin*, 1.26.27.

is a brief but true definition of virtue to say, it is the order of love."[47] Since the definition of true virtue is love, and as we have seen in the previous chapter, only God can restore man to true virtue, this implies that only God can create in man true ordered love. Consequently, as we have seen, the same concept is applied to righteousness and justification. Augustine's idea of the impossibility of true love independently of externally given righteousness is the logical conclusion of Augustine's uncompromising position regarding the impossibility of virtue apart from divine grace.[48] Also in this thesis, the Augustinian basis of Luther's *Heidelberg Disputation* stands inasmuch as, also for Augustine, the love of God (the Holy Spirit) creates in man that which is pleasing to God rather than looking for a love that man autonomously produces.

The following question may be raised: Since it is apparent that not everyone has this faith, why does God give this gift only to some and not to others? Certainly, it is clear that not everybody has faith. Augustine answered this question with his long and detailed treatment of divine predestination. This matter is extensively discussed especially in *On the Predestination of the Saints* and *On the Gift of Perseverance*, but we find careful explanation of this idea also in many other Augustinian works.[49] Even though not explicitly mentioned, predestination is strongly implied throughout the entire *Heidelberg Disputation*. Man always reacts violently to such an idea, to the idea of a God who is free to deliver and justify only some from the bondage into which man has plunged himself. "Arbitrariness," "unrighteousness," "unfairness," "favoritism": these are some of the

47. Augustine, *The City of God*, 15.22.

48. "Your past works indeed, before you believed, were either none, or if they seemed good, were nothing worth. For if they were none, you were as a man without feet, or with sore feet unable to walk: but if they seemed good, before you believed, you ran indeed, but by running aside from the way you went astray instead of coming to the goal. It is for us, then, both to run, and to run in the way. He that runs aside from the way, runs to no purpose, or rather runs but to toil. He goes the more astray, the more he runs aside from the way. What is the way by which we run? Christ has told us, '*I am the Way*' (John 14:6). What the home to which we run? I am the Truth. By Him you run, to Him you run, in Him you rest. But, that we might run by Him, He reached even unto us: for we were afar off, foreigners in a far country. Not enough that we were in a far country, we were feeble also that we could not stir. A Physician, He came to the sick: a Way, He extended Himself to them that were in a far country." Augustine, *First Epistle of John*, 10.1.

49. "How He dispenses those benefits, making some deservedly vessels of wrath, others graciously vessels of mercy—who has known the mind of the Lord, or who has been His counsellor? If, then, we attain to the honour of grace, let us not be ungrateful by attributing to ourselves what we have received. '*For what have we which we have not received?*' (1 Cor 4:7)." Augustine, *Against Two Letters of the Pelagians*, 1.20.38.

terms that usually describe and summarize the typical objections. Independently of a discussion about the accuracy or inaccuracy of these objections, it appears to be true that man is generally inclined to consider his own concept of justice as the highest possible concept of justice, a concept that he also seeks to impose upon God, or to expect from him. On the one hand, man vehemently protests when God demands and works according to his own decree and justice; on the other hand, man always assumes that an omnipotent and absolutely free divine being must work according to those definitions of morality and justice which man has developed by the rational process of his "pure" reason. Expressed in other words, when it comes to predestination, man lays this charge presupposing that there is some kind of independent idea of "righteousness" to which God must adapt himself. However, the Augustinian God is not such a divinity. Such a divinity may meet Plato's conception of the divinity, who conceived of a God who adapts his own being and activity to a number of eternal auto-subsistent ideas. Rather, Augustinianism asserts that God is more than righteous. He *is* righteousness itself. He establishes what is righteous because he *is* righteousness. Man's accusation that an absolutely free God is unrighteous and unfair is grounded on the presupposition that mere man knows what is righteous and what is not.[50]

As will be discussed in the final chapter, Aristotelian, Pelagian, and Kantian moral philosophies, with Leibniz's theodicy, all share the same background and grow out of the same intellectual soil: man must work in order to become righteous, to make himself acceptable in the eyes of God. This is equally true for other philosophies that are grounded in and developed along the same principles of these philosophical positions. The main anthropological presupposition that they share may be summarized as follows: man is naturally good, or at least he is able by himself to become morally good. The result is that Aristotelianism, Pelagianism, and Kantianism reject, explicitly or implicitly, any information given by revelation, insisting instead on their own definition of "moral," "good," and "God."

However, we have seen that Augustinianism is very far from this approach to ethics. Consequently, we will see how the philosophy of the cross is diametrically opposed to any other philosophy that does not have this cross as its starting point. We will discuss the relation of the philosophy of the cross to the nature of the ethical claims behind which man hides a swarm of philosophical rational arguments. Thus, it will be demonstrated how the Aristotelian, Pelagian, Kantian, and Leibnizian views of

---

50. Augustine, *Against Two Letters of the Pelagians*, 2.7.13; *The City of God*, 21.12.

righteousness are utterly reversed by Luther. Man is not righteous by himself. He does not become righteous by a life of good works, or by the mere acceptance of and conformity to the moral law. Rather, man is declared righteous by a supernatural and graciously free act of God which he performs according to his eternal decree of predestination. Man's works do not make him righteous. According to Luther's Augustinian philosophy of the cross, true righteousness is the necessary prerequisite for producing good works.

Luther believed that the philosophy of the cross reveals and unmasks the ethical presuppositions and demands of natural reason under which man hides as the pretext for a supposed objective and unbiased rationality. However, so far I have not given any evidence for my claim. But we are approaching a demonstration of these assertions. The substantial influence that Augustine had on Luther has been instrumental in demonstrating the level of harmony of thought between two of the main founders of western civilization. Accordingly, the research will seek to demonstrate how western philosophy, through two of its representative thinkers, has radically and utterly rejected the legacy of Augustine and Luther regarding theology and moral philosophy. The last section of the *Heidelberg Disputation* which we will discuss will be essential for the setting forth of this argument of philosophy of religion. It is the very core of Luther's theses. The theology of glory and the theology of the cross are the two poles of Luther's argument. As the reader has already seen, by the "philosophy of the cross" we mean the Augustinian message of Luther's *Heidelberg Disputation*, while by the "philosophy of glory" we refer to those philosophies and theologies which are grounded on Aristotelianism or Pelagianism. We will see what the philosophy of the cross is, and what the philosophy of glory is. Moreover, we will discuss the philosophical thesis that can be deduced from the *Heidelberg Disputation*: every secular philosophy developed apart from Christianity may be classified as a theology of glory. At the same time, we will study the Augustinian ground of this claim.

CHAPTER 5

THE GLORY AND THE CROSS

Is IT POSSIBLE TO draw a parallel between Augustine and Luther from a text which is as peculiar among all the works of Luther as *Heidelberg Disputation*, theses 19–24? After all, Luther mentions Augustine explicitly and frequently in other writings, as for example in his commentary on the epistle of Paul to the Romans and in his *The Bondage of the Will*, while Augustine does not explicitly appear in theses 19–24. Moreover, the concepts and the original language of this section of the *Heidelberg Disputation* appear to be absent from earlier theological and philosophical works. Certainly, Luther employs the terminology in question to communicate a highly original message. Is this true also with respect to the presence of Augustine in these theses? What is the role of the African bishop in theses 19–24, the core of Luther's disputation?

While reading the works of Luther in preparation for this paper, the writer encountered several passages which remind him rather vividly of Augustine's language and ideas. We must remember that Luther read and studied Augustine voraciously while he was a canon, both because of his own personal interest and because of the dedication of his religious order to the study of Augustine's works. As a young professor of theology appointed at the university of Wittenberg, he also revised the curriculum, replacing scholastic theology and philosophy with Augustine as a complement to Biblical studies and exegesis. As we have already seen, Augustine was a crucial milestone during the early part of his career. This is one of the reasons which explain the presence of similarities also in this section of the *Heidelberg Disputation*.

This chapter will do what has already been done with respect to the previous sections of the *Heidelberg Disputation*: it will attempt to demonstrate the Augustinian nature and ground of Luther's theses. One of the main points of these theses is the humanity of Christ. This topic includes the necessity of the bodily incarnation of the Logos, and the impossibility of a true knowledge of God if this incarnation is bypassed. In this regard, we will see that what a famous Lutheran scholar has written is not true, namely, that "for Augustine it [the necessity to know God in the man Jesus] is only one point among many others."[1] On the contrary, the incarnation with the consequent humanity of the Logos is an essential point for Augustine, not only for his theology as such, but also for his philosophy. For this reason, we will see that Luther is right to place Augustine among the theologians of the cross. At the same time, Augustine will be seen to be opposed to those scholars whom Luther calls "theologians of glory."

We will also study how Luther's objections to the adversaries of his day resemble the objections of Augustine to his counterparts, that is, the Platonists and Pelagians. It may be objected that there is no real connection between the Platonists and Pelagians. However, according to Augustinianism, these two groups are connected to each other by a theoretical common denominator. In fact, they all explicitly (like the Platonists) or implicitly (like the Pelagians and the Scholastics) reject God's revelation, that is, the incarnation of the Logos and his humiliation, cross and resurrection, with the theoretical and ethical implications of this dogma.

Theses 19–28 constitute the core of the *Heidelberg Disputation*. This chapter is introductory to the philosophical analysis that will follow in the concluding chapter, where we will explore the antithesis between the Christian philosophy of the cross and the secular philosophy of glory.

> *19. That person does not deserve to be called a theologian who looks upon the "invisible" things of God as though they were clearly "perceptible in those things which have actually happened" (Rom 1:20; cf. 1 Cor 1:21–25).*[2]

---

1. Althaus, *Luther*, 183.

2. "This is apparent in the example of those who were 'theologians' and still were called 'fools' by the Apostle in Rom 1:22. Furthermore, the invisible things of God are virtue, godliness, wisdom, justice, goodness, and so forth. The recognition of all these things does not make one worthy or wise." Luther, *Heidelberg*, Proof 19.

The incarnation of the Word, with his cross and resurrection, presupposes and implies the concepts discussed in the previous chapters. This is true not only for Luther, but also for Augustine. Luther's *Heidelberg Disputation* is a set of theological theses which are all interconnected and which should be read as an organic whole. However, this is true also of Augustine's theology of grace. For the African theologian, the necessity of the incarnation and of the cross[3] presupposes and implies the bondage of man's will.[4] The bondage of the will implies the uselessness of "good works" without grace and the necessity of God's gracious operation to enable man to perform good works[5] with the necessity of external righteousness obtained by grace alone through faith alone.[6] Furthermore, the incarnation is also an evidence of God's sovereign predestination.[7]

In order to understand the content of thesis 19, it is necessary to be familiar with Luther's understanding of the Biblical passage which he mentions in the proof of the thesis. In Romans 1:19–20,[8] Paul teaches that man has an innate knowledge of the existence of God, which is derived from creation, including man's created conscience. This general knowledge is attainable by mere reason, using non-Lutheran terminology. For the Paul of Luther, real atheists do not exist inasmuch as atheists are unable to deny God's existence, and when they do so they are actually denying God's authority, not his existence. This is in harmony with the following passage which Luther quotes in the proof, 1 Cor 1:21–25.[9] In fact, in Rom 1:20 Paul teaches that man is aware of the "power" and "Godhead" of God, that

3. Augustine, *On the Trinity*, 13.13.

4. *Ibid.*, 13.16; *The Gospel of John*, 3.12–13.

5. Augustine, *Reply to Faustus the Manichaean*, 19.7.

6. Augustine, *Enchiridion*, 14.49–19.51.

7. Augustine, *On the Predestination of the Saints*, 30; *Enchiridion*, 36. For more Augustinian passages on these topics, see the previous chapters. I mention these specific passages because they show to a certain degree the *relationship* which exists between these doctrines and the cross in the theology of Augustine.

8. "Because that which may be known of God is manifest in them; for God hath shewed it unto them. For the invisible things of him from the creation of the world are clearly seen, being understood by the things that are made, even his eternal power and Godhead; so that they are without excuse." Rom 1:19–20.

9. "For after that in the wisdom of God the world by wisdom knew not God, it pleased God by the foolishness of preaching to save them that believe. For the Jews require a sign, and the Greeks seek after wisdom: But we preach Christ crucified, unto the Jews a stumblingblock, and unto the Greeks foolishness; But unto them which are called, both Jews and Greeks, Christ the power of God, and the wisdom of God. Because the foolishness of God is wiser than men; and the weakness of God is stronger than men." 1 Cor 1:21–25.

is, of his omnipotence and his divine holiness. However, he is unable to know more beyond these two divine qualities. The man who recognizes God's omnipotence and holiness through *general* or *superficial* knowledge does not know that this God reveals himself in history in certain ways, i.e., he does not have a *proper* or *inside* knowledge of the Divinity. Man does not possess this special revelation because this knowledge cannot be understood from creation. To be more specific, man does not know that God, in his word as the second person of the Trinity, became incarnate in Jesus Christ as God's highest revelation. Moreover, according to Paul, man misuses this general revelation from creation, and he abuses this knowledge in order to produce his own forms of idolatrous religion and to develop his own philosophical ideas (Rom 1:21–25).[10]

Now, according to Luther, to know "the invisible things of God" is not epistemologically or ethically profitable. This knowledge surely has its importance, but to know and to investigate the "virtue, godliness, wisdom, justice, goodness"[11] of God in themselves does not permit man to achieve his highest philosophical, theological and existential end, that is, a general knowledge of God "does not make one worthy or wise."[12] This general knowledge is a good thing in itself, but by itself it does not enlighten a man or make him virtuous. This is because also the "wise of this world," those who are outside the sphere of God's special revelation, know these things. These "fools," as Paul and Luther call them, can grasp these attributes of God. However, they are "fools" because they bypass an absolutely necessary spiritual and enlightening principle: the revelation of God in the flesh. This revelation is essential in order properly to understand the attributes of God as considered in his saving relation to mankind.

---

10. It may be helpful to read a comment of Luther himself. Here, he explains the two verses together: "The meaning therefore is this: Even if the wise of this world should be unable to perceive that the world is created, they could perceive the invisible things of God in the works of the created world if, namely, they were to regard these works that witness to God, as word and Scripture. 'For seeing that in the wisdom of God the world through its wisdom knew not God, it was God's pleasure through the foolishness of the preaching to save them that believe' (1 Cor 1:21). This interpretation seems to be contradicted by the fact that the text says that they knew God, but the difficulty is readily solved by what we read a little farther on: Even if they knew God, 'they refused to have God in their knowledge,' i.e., by their actions they gave themselves the appearance of knowing him." Luther, *Romans*, 20-21. See Althaus, *Luther*, 15–19 for an excellent treatment of the difference between "general" or "superficial" knowledge of God and "proper" or "inside" knowledge of God.

11. Luther, *Heidelberg*, Proof 20.

12. *Ivi.*

It is clear that Luther's main targets are the Scholastic theologians of his day. He viewed Scholasticism as lost in a tangled system of Aristotelian definitions which did not allow one to get to the core of the Christian message. In opposition to this, Luther presents his philosophically iconoclastic theology of the cross, which is deeply rooted in the Scriptures and in Augustine, not in Aristotelianism or Pelagianism. Since we are studying the Augustinian ground of Luther's thought, the pertinent questions are these: do we find a similar polemical approach also in Augustine? In which sense can we say that thesis 19 of the *Heidelberg Disputation* is Augustinian in nature?

We find Augustine saying similar things to a group of philosophers whom he seemed to know well: the Platonists. It is not my intention here to deny or discuss in detail the Platonist elements of Augustine's thought. Nor I am necessarily implying that Luther specifically had in mind Augustine's criticism of Platonism when he wrote this section of the disputation. Nevertheless, Augustine uses very similar language against the Platonists on several occasions. More importantly, he addresses in the Platonists a similar error that Luther addresses in his theological adversaries in thesis 19. Luther condemned the Scholastics because they wanted to know God while avoiding his incarnation and the cross, with all the doctrines implied by the cross, such as the bondage of the will, and the absolute necessity of grace. Similarly, Augustine sharply critiques the intellectual pride of the Platonists who did not acknowledge that the divine Logos whom they superficially grasped with their intellect has revealed himself in human flesh, namely, in Jesus Christ.

Augustine recognizes the superiority of the Platonists[13] among the philosophers: "we prefer these to all other philosophers, and confess that they approach nearest to us."[14] Nevertheless, Augustine contends that this knowledge of the "invisible things" of God has brought the Platonists no profit. On the contrary, this knowledge has made them more ethically

---

13. Augustine was not aware of the modern distinction between "Platonism" and "Neo-Platonism." Augustine read mainly Plotinus and Porphyry, and for him they were simply Platonists. See Harrison, *Augustine*, 11–15.

14. "Whatever philosophers, therefore, thought concerning the supreme God, that He is both the maker of all created things, the light by which things are known, and the good in reference to which things are to be done; that we have in Him the first principle of nature, the truth of doctrine, and the happiness of life—whether these philosophers may be more suitably called Platonists, or whether they may give some other name to their sect . . . we prefer these to all other philosophers, and confess that they approach nearest to us." Augustine, *The City of God*, 8.9.

proud and intellectually foolish.[15] The reason is that they did not recognize the Christological goal which is the end of the superficial knowledge of God. Platonists understood that God is the creator, the light of all knowledge, the source of good and that every man receives from him being, true knowledge, and a life of happiness.[16] For Augustine, however, even though these concepts are very important,[17] they are not epistemologically, and therefore ethically, sufficient. The Trinity of God, the incarnation of the Logos with his life, death, and resurrection, the atonement, and so on, are totally absent from their writings.[18] Augustine goes even so far as to insist that the Platonists oppose these distinctively Christian truths.[19] These points are not of secondary importance to Augustine with his distinctively Christological philosophy. In fact, Augustine, as well as Luther, employs very strong language against those who despise or ignore the incarnation of the Word, who is the Logos through which the entire universe was created and is sustained. The Word is the *medium* for the right knowledge of everything. Nevertheless, Platonists have seen this Logos only from afar. They have not grasped or acknowledged that the Logos has manifested himself in human flesh, and this is due to the impossibility of mankind to know God through mere intellectual or moral efforts.

Augustine's sermons on the Gospel of John contain several places where Augustine criticizes the Platonists for making the same kind of mistake that Luther saw in his adversaries. This collection of sermons contains a significant number of sections where Augustine argues for the absolute

15. "Where it has been said by him, '*that God has manifested to them by those things which are made His invisible things, that they might be seen by the understanding*' (Rom 1:20), there it has also been said that they did not rightly worship God Himself, because they paid divine honors, which are due to Him alone, to other things also to which they ought not to have paid them . . . the apostle would have us understand him as meaning the Romans, and Greeks, and Egyptians, who gloried in the name of wisdom." *Ibid.*, 8.10.1.

16. *Ibid.*, 8.9.

17. Augustine himself defines the reading of the Platonists as providential for his intellectual deliverance from the Manichean materialistic idea of the divinity. "You [i.e., God] procured for me, by the instrumentality of one inflated with most monstrous pride, certain books of the Platonists, translated from Greek into Latin." Augustine, *Confessions*, 7.9.13. Also in this section, however, Augustine sets the intellectual pride of the Platonists against the divine humility of the incarnated Word.

18. Augustine, *Confessions*, 7.9.3, 19.25, 21.27.

19. "I have been rightly displeased, too, with the praise with which I extolled Plato or the Platonists or the Academic philosophers [Augustine is referring to his *Against the Academicians* 2.10.24; 3.17.37–18, 41] beyond what was proper for such irreligious men, especially those against whose great errors Christian teaching must be defended." Augustine, *Retractions*, 1.1.4.

necessity of an intellectual understanding and ethical acceptance of the humility of God's incarnation in the man Jesus Christ. This is often done, as it has been said, in the context of polemics with the "proud" Platonists. One passage stresses Augustine's view on the matter even more. It is quite lengthy but worthy of quotation inasmuch as it constitutes a good summary of the claim that has been made here, that is, the presence of the Augustinian principle of the absolute necessity of the incarnate God in Luther's thought.

> But truly there have been some philosophers of this world who have sought for the Creator by means of the creature; for He can be found by means of the creature, as the apostle plainly says, "*For the invisible things of Him from the creation of the world are clearly seen, being understood by the things that are made, even His eternal power and glory; so they are without excuse.*" And it follows, "*Because that, when they knew God;*" he did not say, Because they did not know, but "*Because that, when they knew God, they glorified Him not as God, neither were thankful; but became vain in their imaginations, and their foolish heart was darkened.*" How darkened? It follows, when he says more plainly: "*Professing themselves to be wise, they became fools*" (Rom 1:20–22). They saw whither they must come; but ungrateful to Him who afforded them what they saw, they wished to ascribe to themselves what they saw; and having become proud, they lost what they saw, and were turned from it to idols and images, and to the worship of demons, to adore the creature and to despise the Creator. But these having been blinded did those things, and became proud, that they might be blinded: when they were proud they said that they were wise. Those, therefore, concerning whom he said, "*Who, when they had known God,*" saw this which John says, that by the Word of God all things were made. For these things are also found in the books of the philosophers: and that God has an only-begotten Son, by whom are all things. They were able to see that which is, but they saw it from afar: they were unwilling to hold the lowliness of Christ, in which ship they might have arrived in safety at that which they were able to see from afar and the cross of Christ appeared vile to them. The sea has to be crossed, and do you despise the wood? Oh, proud wisdom! You laugh to scorn the crucified Christ; it is He whom you see from afar: "*In the beginning was the Word, and the Word was with God.*" But wherefore was He crucified? Because the wood of His humiliation was needful to you. . . . be carried by the wood: believe in the crucified One,

and you shall arrive there. On account of you He was crucified, to teach you humility; and because if He should come as God, He would not be recognized. For if He should come as God, He would not come to those who were not able to see God. For not according to His Godhead does He either come or depart; since He is everywhere present, and is contained in no place. But, according to what did He come? He appeared as a man.[20]

For the Platonists, both the idea of an incarnate Divinity and the idea of a bodily resurrection are foolishness. For them, man reaches the Divinity by becoming divine. It is absurd that the Divinity should reach man by becoming like him. A divine being would never defile himself with base material flesh. This intellectual objection of the Platonists falls under the same category of the error that Luther ascribes to his intellectual adversaries. The difference is that, while Platonists reject the incarnation itself with its implications, Luther's adversaries deny the implication of this incarnation, even though they formally maintain such dogma. Therefore, the Augustinian spirit of Luther's theses is still recognizable after careful analysis. We saw in the previous chapter that Luther is Augustinian is his theology of the absolute dependence of man upon God. Now, we see the Augustinianism of Luther concerning the absolute necessity of a human-divine mediator.

We now understand better another aspect of the meaning of the expressions "theology of glory" and "theology of the cross." Luther says that, in order to know God, intellectual knowledge and ethical acceptance of the cross of Christ are necessary. This is because God wills to reveal himself and to be known firstly in the cross. A person who does this is a theologian of the cross because he bases his theological philosophy on the cross. On the contrary, a theologian of glory bypasses the cross of Christ either by denying it or rejecting the theological doctrines that it includes. Therefore, they want to see God in his glory, without passing through the cross of Christ which is, for Luther and Augustine, a necessary intellectual and personal experience. They are "theologians of glory" because they skip the cross of Christ in order to attain the essential glory of God. From the perspective of Luther's Augustinian philosophy of the cross, however, this is unprofitable, because it is not the way in which the Divinity is pleased to make himself known.

---

20. Augustine, *The Gospel of John*, 2.4. See also *Ibid.*, 2.2–3; 2.16; 3.15; 10.1. *First Epistle of John*, 3.6; 4.4.

20. He deserves to be called a theologian, however, who compre-
hends the visible and manifest things of God seen through suffer-
ing and the cross.[21]

We turn now to thesis 20, which strengthens the previous thesis, since it is actually its positive version. In fact, thesis 19 tells us what a theologian *must not* do, while thesis 20 explains positively what a theologian *must* do. It is necessary to make a few preliminary remarks before we begin to analyze it. Firstly, we must not be misled by the structure of the *Heidelberg Disputation*. Luther is not referring exclusively to the doctrine of the saving work of Christ in general and his cross in particular, that is, to the general topic of theses 19–24. If this were true, Luther's criticism of his contemporary colleagues would be rather unmotivated. This section of the *Heidelberg Disputation* must be read with the other sections in mind which have already been discussed, that is, it must be read in its context. In chapter 2, we have seen that man is totally unable and unwilling to know God properly. Chapter 3 has established that man's "good" works apart from grace are nothing but evil deeds. Chapter 4 has shown how true righteousness is obtained by electing grace alone through faith alone. This is the context of theses 19–24, all of which is implied in the word "cross." The theology of the cross mentioned in thesis 21 and 24 is the message of the *Heidelberg Disputation* as a whole. Without this theology of the absolute grace of God before us, these sections would not make much sense.

In the proof of thesis 20 we meet again the concept of *deus abscon-ditus*. According to this idea, God is pleased to reveal his glory and power hidden under shame and weakness. In Christ, God has concealed his

21 "The manifest and visible things of God are placed in opposition to the invisible, namely, his human nature, weakness, foolishness. The Apostle in 1 Cor 1:25 calls them the weakness and folly of God. Because men misused the knowledge of God through works, God wished again to be recognized in suffering, and to condemn "wisdom concerning invisible things" by means of "wisdom concerning visible things," so that those who did not honor God as manifested in his works should honor him as he is hidden in his suffering (*absconditum in passionibus*). As the Apostle says in 1 Cor 1:21, 'For since, in the wisdom of God, the world did not know God through wisdom, it pleased God through the folly of what we preach to save those who believe.' Now it is not sufficient for anyone, and it does him no good to recognize God in his glory and majesty, unless he recognizes him in the humility and shame of the cross. Thus God destroys the wisdom of the wise, as Isa 45:15 says, 'Truly, thou art a God who hidest thyself.' So, also, in John 14:8, where Philip spoke according to the theology of glory: 'Show us the Father.' Christ forthwith set aside his flighty thought about seeing God elsewhere and led him to himself, saying, 'Philip, he who has seen me has seen the Father' (John 14:9). For this reason true theology and recognition of God are in the crucified Christ, as it is also stated in John 10 (John 14:6) 'No one comes to the Father, but by me.' 'I am the door' (John 10:9), and so forth." Luther, *Heidelberg*, Proof 20.

glorious divinity under weak human flesh. Moreover, as we have seen, the *deus absconditus* is combined with the *sub contra specie* principle, about which Luther states that "the manifest and visible things of God are placed in *opposition* to the invisible, namely, his human nature, weakness, foolishness."[22]

Luther claims that man is naturally prone to give preeminence to works, while God will be known and recognized in the suffering of the cross. The topic of works reappears here, which has been much discussed previously, especially in chapter 3 where theses 1–12 have been examined. However, the word "works" is ambiguous: it may refer to "works" in the sense of virtuous deeds, or it may mean the works of creation from which man achieves a general but non enlightening knowledge of God. Whatever Luther meant exactly, his main idea is clear. Man misuses both the insufficient general knowledge of God (works of creation) and the desire for a moral life (virtuous works) in order to neglect God hidden in the weakness and foolishness of the cross. A true theologian, on the contrary, knows that the humiliation of the incarnate Logos is actually the way God is pleased to give his highest revelation. He thus deserves to be called a theologian because he opposes the unprofitable glory of works with the saving humility of the cross.

In order to understand the Augustinian character of this thesis, we must establish the second premise on a specific word which appears to be of secondary importance but which is actually very significant. The word in question is "manifest," which is the English translation of the Latin "posterior," the word which Luther uses in the original Latin text of the *Heidelberg Disputation*.[23] Luther is referring to a Biblical event reported in the book of Exodus. In fact, the word "posteriora mea" is the expression found in the Vulgate translation of Exod 33:23.[24] After the idolatry committed by the people of Israel with the golden calf, a discouraged Moses asks God to show him his glory, that is, to appear to him. God's answer is as follows: "Non poteris videre faciem meam; non enim videbit me homo et vivet . . . Ecce, inquit, est locus apud me, stabis super petram; cumque transibit gloria mea, ponam te in foramine petrae et protegam dextera mea, donec transeam; tollamque manum meam, et videbis *posteriora mea*; faciem autem meam videre non poteris."[25]

---

22. *Ivi.* Emphasis added.

23. Forde, *On Being a Theologian of the Cross*, 78.

24. *Vulgate Bible.*

25. *Ivi.* Emphasis added. "Thou canst not see my face: for there shall no man see

Luther is drawing a parallel between God's showing his "back parts" to Moses and the cross of Christ. As Moses was not allowed to see God directly but only indirectly, at the same time no one is allowed or able to know God in the fullness of his glory. This means that man is unable to receive a vision of God of what he is in himself, that is, of his attributes as such, as Moses wished. Man cannot know God except through the "humility and shame of the cross."[26] He needs a mediation and a mediator, and this mediator has revealed himself in "human nature, weakness, foolishness."[27] Therefore, the "back parts" of God that Moses saw are, according to Luther, a prophetic representation of the human nature taken by the second person of the Trinity in Jesus Christ; on the other hand, the "glory" of God that Moses wanted to see is for Luther an example of that "theology of glory" which fails to understand the absolute necessity of the mediating incarnation. Theologically speaking, the "back parts" of God are a prefiguring figure, or type, of the future incarnation of the Word.

We find the same concept expressed by Luther in Augustine's *On the Trinity*. Far from being a secondary point, the humanity of Christ, the revelation of God in the flesh, is a milestone in the entirety of Augustine's philosophy and theology. The philosophical centrality of the incarnation is not an exaggeration or a misunderstanding. In fact, it has been said that Augustine's treatise of the Trinity "seeks to understand and to model what Christian life is all about,"[28] being "a new *Hortensius*, completely revised on *Christological* and Trinitarian grounds."[29] This point can never be emphasized enough.

First of all, Augustine insists that to see the face of God, i.e., God as he is in himself, would be to claim to behold the invisible and eternal God in his divine nature, which no creature can see and live. Even Moses was excluded from the possibility of obtaining such a privilege: "this was not granted to him, even though he desired it; who will dare to say, that by the like forms which had appeared visibly to him also, not the creature serving God, but that itself which is God, appeared to the eyes of a mortal man?"[30]

---

me, and live . . . Behold, there is a place by me, and thou shalt stand upon a rock: And it shall come to pass, while my glory passeth by, that I will put thee in a clift of the rock, and will cover thee with my hand while I pass by: And I will take away mine hand, and thou shalt see my back parts: but my face shall not be seen." Exod 33:20–23.

26. Luther, *Heidelberg*, Proof 20.

27. *Ivi.*

28. Levering, *The Theology of Augustine*, 152.

29. *Ibid.*, 185. Emphasis added.

30. Augustine, *On the Trinity*, 2.16.27.

To prove this, the African thinker goes on to quote Exodus 33:20–23, the passage which was quoted earlier in reference to thesis 20.[31] Augustine calls this immediate vision the "face of God," or "form of God."[32] Rather, God showed Moses only his "back parts." Augustine interprets these "back parts" figuratively in the same way that Luther does: "His back parts are to be taken to be his flesh, in which he was born of the Virgin, and died, and rose again; whether they are called back parts on account of the posteriority of mortality, or because it was almost in the end of the world, that is, at a late period, that he deigned to take it."[33] Moreover, for Augustine, as for Luther, this approach is not optional. In fact, he goes on to say that to approach God in this way of the incarnation is the only correct way. This is because God has decided this to be the main step in the economy of salvation: "we ought to see the back parts of Christ, that is his flesh."[34] Christ is the Word of God in the flesh, and during this earthly life he wants to be known not in his eternal glory, but in his fleshy revelation, "God latent in weakness."[35]

When Augustine talks about "the back parts of Christ" in *On the Trinity*, he is expressing the same concept that Luther is expounding in thesis 20. For Augustine and Luther, man cannot know God in his divine nature as such if he does not recognize first the human nature in which the Word has revealed himself. Augustine and Luther conduct the same typological exegesis of Exodus 33:23. The idea that flows from their exegesis is the same: the absolute necessity of the incarnation in order to know God not only generally or superficially, but also properly and inwardly. Philosophically speaking, the incarnation of the Logos is necessary not only for mere epistemological reasons and purposes, but also for ethical reasons and purposes. Bypassing this principle, according to Augustine the theologian falls into pride[36] or, to use Luther's words, he is not even worthy "to be called a theologian."[37]

From this follows that metaphysics is certainly possible, both for Augustine and for Luther. As we have seen, natural man is not entirely ignorant of God. However, when man focuses on the question of general

---

31. *Ibid.*, 2.16.28.
32. *Ibid.*, 2.17.
33. *Ivi.*
34. *Ivi.*
35. Augustine, *The Gospel of John*, 4.4.
36. *Ibid.*, 2.1–4.
37. Luther, *Heidelberg*, Thesis 19.

metaphysics, he makes the same mistake that Luther's Augustinianism condemns. First of all, it would be helpful to summarize and clarify Luther's theological anthropology. When Luther teaches (in harmony with Augustine and Calvin, and with Christian thought in general) that man in his fallenness has become *ethically* corrupt, he is not making a "mechanical" argument. He is not saying that man does not have the tool to know God, so that his knowledge of God is fallacious. The argument is more *ethical*, intended as a living relationship between man and God. Natural man hates God, and "hatred" is something ethical. In order to hate someone, one must have some knowledge of that someone. In fact, as we have already discussed, man has a *general* or *superficial* knowledge of God. Nevertheless, men "by their unrighteousness suppress the truth" (Rom 1:18, a verse which both Augustine and Luther often quote and on which they comment). This means that this superficial knowledge or general metaphysics is insufficient. Furthermore, man, by misusing this general metaphysics, rejects the proper knowledge of the Divinity. This is why it has been said that our discourse is mainly *ethical*, for man is corrupt in his ethics, intended both as ethical presuppositions and man's own ethical constitution of nature. A wrong epistemology is the result. But "wrong" does not mean that man is *absolutely* and *in every single respect* always *totally* unable to talk about religion or God. He has the capacity, but he cannot do so in the *right* way and he cannot reach the *right* conclusion and the *final* end.

Concerning the possibility of metaphysics, neither Luther nor Augustine hold that, since this is man's ethical condition, he is unable to *know* or even to *think* or *talk* about God *at all*. Nor are they saying that men are not able to understand this falleness *intellectually*. Luther writes that "the natural light of reason is strong enough to regard God as good, gracious, merciful, and generous."[38] But for the German thinker, this general knowledge is insufficient. Also for the African theologian, this general knowledge is insufficient, which is evident from Augustine's criticism of the Platonic rejection of the Incarnation. Luther, like Augustine, acknowledges metaphysics. The problem is exactly that for Luther, as for Augustine, to focus on mere metaphysics implies that we fall into what Luther is trying to reject, that is, the theology of glory. Expressed in other words, when we underline the importance of metaphysics we are approaching the error that Luther's philosophy of the cross condemns. This focus on metaphysics is, for Luther, abstract and incomplete, to say the least. This is

38. Quoted in Althaus, *Luther*, 16.

due to the fact that this metaphysics does not tell me what God is *for me*, what he wants *from me*, and *what I owe to him* (Augustine says, generally, the same things, when he stresses the absolute necessity of the Incarnation against both the Platonists and Pelagians. I explained this in the fifth chapter). This metaphysics is mere speculative thought, totally detached from a living relational knowledge of God. Actually, it is not totally detached from practical life, for this metaphysical knowledge is related to practical ethics, but in a negative sense. In fact, man misuses this metaphysical knowledge, falling into proud intellectual speculation (Platonism) or into the moral pride of legalism and moralism (Pelagianism and Scholasticism). Thus, metaphysics is possible, but it is not the *goal*. It is surely a point worthy of mention, but it is not *the* point. In fact, this metaphysics (*general* or *superficial* knowledge of God) must be directed to the theology of the cross (*proper* or *inside* knowledge of God), which is the reason why Luther argues in the proof of thesis 19 that the recognition of these things (metaphysics) does not make a man worthy or wise, that is, *saved* or *enlightened*. Metaphysics is possible, but it is not an end in itself: the cross is. In this sense, also Augustine is radically anti-metaphysical, because he asserts the absolute necessity of the incarnation and of the cross, with an essential stress on revelation, for any *proper* and *inside* knowledge of God.

> 21. *A theology of glory calls evil good and good evil. A theology of the cross calls the thing what it actually is.*[39]

In the previous thesis, Luther claimed that those who do not acknowledge God both revealed and hidden in the man Jesus Christ inevitably seek to know God and to please him through works. In thesis 20, by works are meant both virtuous deeds and the works of creation which witness of God. In thesis 21, however, the context is more explicit and it seems specifically to address "works" as virtuous deeds: "they hate the cross and suffering and love works and the glory of works . . . impossible for a person

---

39. "This is clear: He who does not know Christ does not know God hidden in suffering. Therefore he prefers works to suffering, glory to the cross, strength to weakness, wisdom to folly, and, in general, good to evil. These are the people whom the apostle calls 'enemies of the cross of Christ' (Phil 3:18), for they hate the cross and suffering and love works and the glory of works. Thus they call the good of the cross evil and the evil of a deed good. God can be found only in suffering and the cross, as has already been said Therefore the friends of the cross say that the cross is good and works are evil, for through the cross works are dethroned and the 'old Adam,' who is especially edified by works, is crucified. It is impossible for a person not to be puffed up by his 'good works' unless he has first been deflated and destroyed by suffering and evil until he knows that he is worthless and that his works are not his but God's." Luther, *Heidelberg*, Proof 21.

not to be puffed up by his 'good works' unless he has first been deflated and destroyed by suffering and evil until he knows that he is worthless and that his works are not his but God's."[40]

To deny the revelation of God in Jesus Christ means adopting an upside down epistemology, not only with respect to theology as such, but also with respect to ethics. According to Luther, those who bypass the cross of Christ call "evil good and good evil."[41] This means that instead of the cross of Christ, the event which displays the absolutely sovereign grace of God, they prefer the meritorious system of good works. It really does not matter very much if the "works" that Luther addresses are the Platonic drift from the divinity to idolatry because of intellectual pride, the Pelagian theology, or the secular Kantian philosophy of religion. Luther insists that when a man does not recognize the cross, his only other option is works. Whether this legalistic system of works consists in the pious deeds prescribed by whatever ecclesiastical authority or by the moral philosophical imperatives of the purity of motive, the fact is that the cross of Christ is rejected.

Both the reason and the fruit of this rejection are pride. Luther describes this pride as calling "evil good and good evil."[42] Thus, the cross is explicitly called evil by the Platonists by their denial of divine incarnation, and implicitly called evil by Pelagians and Scholastics by their legalistic theology of works. On the contrary, a proper understanding of God's revelation in the cross generates the greatest humility. To express the same concept with Luther's words, the "theology of the cross calls the thing what it actually is."[43] The theologian of the cross has been ethically destroyed in his intellectual attempt to find a way to God through mere contemplation or through independent moral virtues. He sees that, as Christ humiliated himself even though he was God incarnate, he must refuse all the demands of independence of his supposed reason as influenced and guided by his fallen ethical nature.

In light of these considerations, we see that a similar analysis of the Platonism of the previous thesis may be made also of the theological adversaries of Augustine and Luther, the Pelagians and Scholastics respectively. We must remember that, according to Luther, the Scholastics of his time were basically Pelagian in their theology.[44] However, since we are

40. *Ivi.*

41. *Ivi.*

42. *Ivi.*

43. *Ivi.*

44. "If it is said of the Scripture passages, 'Return to me . . . and I will return to you'

investigating the Augustinian basis of the *Heidelberg Disputation*, we will focus mainly on Pelagianism. The Pelagians found significant intellectual difficulties in understanding Augustine's doctrine of grace. According to their supposedly rational arguments,[45] it is impossible that man's conversion and his good works are both entirely the gifts of God. From their point of view, Augustinianism would destroy man's liberty and make God an arbitrary tyrant.

We will now see in which sense Luther's charge can be applied also to Augustine's Pelagian adversaries. The Pelagians, with the Manicheans and Donatists, are the group of people whom Augustine most criticized during his lifetime. We may see some points in common between the Pelagian and the Scholastic adversaries of Luther. The Pelagians, as well as the Platonists, are enamored by "virtue, godliness, wisdom, justice, goodness, and so forth." Pelagians and Scholastics take these "invisible things of God" as such, they speculate moralistically about them, and they try to work and live accordingly in order to reflect these attributes in their own moral conduct and philosophy. There is here the key connection between the impossibility of knowing God without the mediation of the cross and man's claim to be able to please God through his works. This means that while Platonists deny and despise the very idea of the incarnation of the Logos because they focus only on "virtue, godliness, wisdom, justice, goodness, and so forth," the Pelagians and the Scholastics deny the implications of such a revelation, even though they do not explicitly reject such a dogma. For the former group, it represents mainly but not exclusively an epistemological problem; for the latter, it is mainly but not exclusively an ethical issue. In fact, several times Augustine marks those who deny this epistemology of the incarnation as "enemies of the cross of Christ." This expression is originally Pauline,[46] and is the same expression that Luther uses in the proof of thesis 21.

In connection with this similarity between scholasticism and Pelagianism, Augustine labels the Pelagians as enemies of the cross. More

---

[Zech 1:3], 'Draw near to God and he will draw near to you' [Jas 4:8], "Seek and you will find" [Matt 7:7], 'You will seek me and find me' [Jer 29:13], and the like, that one is by nature, the other by grace, this is no different from asserting what the Pelagians have said." Luther, *Disputation Against Scholastic Theology*, Thesis 28.

45. Augustine rebukes in particular Julian of Eclanum for his pompous and often invalid use of Aristotle's categories. See *Against Julian*, 1.4.12; 2.10.37; 3.2.7; 5.14.51; 6.20.64. With this, Augustine does not intend to disregard Aristotelian logic as such, but only the proud abuse of it.

46. "For many walk, of whom I have told you often, and now tell you even weeping, that they are the enemies of the cross of Christ." Phil 3:18.

importantly, he does so for the same reason that led Luther to call the Scholastics enemies of the cross: their preference of human moral activity to the cross of Christ. According to Pelagianism, the grace of God displayed in the cross of Christ is simply a new law, different from the Old Testament law, a law that enables the hearers to obey God's will according to God's demands. The law, therefore, has a saving, enlightening power in itself.[47] For Augustine, however, the law of God, even though it is the only good and holy model of conduct, has no saving efficacy. The purpose of the law is to command, and to display the sinfulness of man, in order to lead man to the true source of grace, that is, the cross.[48] Therefore, for the African church father it is not a misrepresentation of the Pelagian position to affirm that according to it grace is the law, and the law is grace.[49]

47. "The whole of this dogma of Pelagius, observe, is carefully expressed in these words, and none other, in the third book of his treatise in defence of the liberty of the will, in which he has taken care to distinguish with so great subtlety these three things—the 'capacity,' the 'volition,' and the 'action,' that is, the 'ability,' the 'volition,' and the 'actuality'—that, whenever we read or hear of his acknowledging the assistance of divine grace in order to our avoidance of evil and accomplishment of good—whatever he may mean by the said assistance of grace, whether law and the teaching or any other thing—we are sure of what he says; nor can we run into any mistake by understanding him otherwise than he means. For we cannot help knowing that, according to his belief, it is not our 'volition' nor our 'action' which is assisted by the divine help, but solely our 'capacity' to will and act, which alone of the three, as he affirms, we have of God. As if that faculty were infirm which God Himself placed in our nature; while the other two, which, as he would have it, are our own, are so strong and firm and self-sufficient as to require none of His help! So that He does not help us to will, nor help us to act, but simply helps us to the possibility of willing and acting." Augustine, *On the Grace of Christ and on Original Sin*, 1.5.6.

48. "The apostle, however, holds the contrary, when he says, '*Work out your own salvation with fear and trembling*' (Phil 2:12). And that they might be sure that it was not simply in their being able to work (for this they had already received in nature and in teaching), but in their actual working, that they were divinely assisted, the apostle does not say to them, 'For it is God that works in you to be able,' as if they already possessed volition and operation among their own resources, without requiring His assistance in respect of these two; but he says, '*For it is God which works in you both to will and to perform of His own good pleasure*' (Phil 2:13) or, as the reading runs in other copies, especially the Greek, '*both to will and to operate.*' Consider, now, whether the apostle did not thus long before foresee by the Holy Ghost that there would arise adversaries of the grace of God; and did not therefore declare that God works within us those two very things, even '*willing*' and '*operating,*' which this man so determined to be our own, as if they were in no wise assisted by the help of divine grace." *Ivi.*

49. "Why, therefore, do those very vain and perverse Pelagians say that the law is the grace of God by which we are helped not to sin? Do they not, by making such an allegation, unhappily and beyond all doubt contradict the great apostle? He, indeed, says, that by the law sin received strength against man; and that man, by the commandment, although it be holy, and just, and good, nevertheless dies, and that death works

This is the reason why Augustine considers the Pelagians enemies of the cross. Like the theological adversaries of Luther, the Pelagians undermine the significance of the cross in order to established a righteousness which is by virtuous works. In several places, Augustine connects this specific charge to the Pelagian overestimation of virtuous works by the law: "Therefore all are enemies of the cross of Christ who, going about to establish their own righteousness, which is of the law—that is, where only the letter commands, and the Spirit does not fulfil—are not subject to the law of God. For if they who are of the law be heirs, faith is made an empty thing. *'If righteousness is by the law, then Christ has died in vain: then is the offense of the cross done away.'* And thus those are enemies of the cross of Christ who say that righteousness is by the law, to which it belongs to command, not to assist. But the grace of God through Jesus Christ the Lord in the Holy Spirit helps our infirmity."[50] As has already been said, this charge is not an overreaction of Augustine, but it is rather he has concluded this upon mature reflection. One may think that, for example, a denial of the bondage of the will as the result of original sin does not necessarily include a denial of the cross of Christ as such. However, according to the African philosopher, this is exactly the case.[51] In fact, for the Augustinianism expounded by Luther's *Heidelberg Disputation*, the cross of Christ presupposes and displays all the theological concepts that have been discussed in the previous sections: the bondage of the will, the impossibility of true virtuous works apart from grace, and the exclusivity of faith for attainment of true righteousness.

For the African thinker, Pelagians are enemies of the cross and, as such, they call evil good and good evil, to use Lutheran language. Their theology, and their consequent ethical position, are upside down.[52] More

---

in him through that which is good, from which death there is no deliverance unless the Spirit quickens him, whom the letter had killed—as he says in another passage, *'The letter kills, but the Spirit gives life'* (2 Cor 3:6) And yet these obstinate persons, blind to God's light, and deaf to His voice, maintain that the letter which kills gives life, and thus gainsay the quickening Spirit." Augustine, *On Grace and Free Will*, 23.11.

50. Augustine, *Against Two Letters of the Pelagians*, 3.7.22. See also *Incomplete Work Against Julian*, 2.198.

51. See Augustine, *Against Two Letters of the Pelagians*, 4.4.8–4.8, and *Incomplete Work Against Julian*, 3.56 for the same charge connected to the Pelagian denial of original sin.

52. "From your self you have the ill doing, from God you have the well doing. On the other hand, see perverse men, how preposterous they are. What they do well, they will needs ascribe to themselves; if they do ill, they will needs accuse God. Reverse this distorted and preposterous proceeding, which puts the thing, as one may say, head downwards, which makes that undermost which is uppermost, and that upwards which

specifically, they attribute saving power to the law of God when the law has actually a deadly power because it accuses man of sinfulness and point to commands that man is not able to fulfill as God requires, i.e., perfectly. On the other hand, this overestimation of the law results in the undermining of the cross of Christ, which is thus reduced to a mere example of perfect moral achievement. Therefore, it is neither an historical nor theoretical decontextualization to contend that also thesis 21 has its main extra-biblical source in Augustine's intellectual polemics against those teachings which fail to ascribe all the merit and all the power of salvation and enlightenment to the sovereign work of God.[53]

> 22. *That wisdom which sees the invisible things of God in works as*
> *perceived by man is completely puffed up, blinded, and hardened.*[54]

As it has been said before, Luther's Christological philosophy is uncompromising. For him, once we attribute even the slightest part of the work of salvation and enlightenment to man, we fall into the unchristian legalist theology of glory (again, this does not mean that man does nothing, but this means that he is neither the *source* nor the *accomplisher* of the light that converts and regenerates his will). When the cross is bypassed, only a moralistic system remains, and we have seen that Luther includes in the same category merely philosophical systems such as Aristotelianism and the more religious ones such as Pelagianism and Scholasticism (we will

---

is downwards." Augustine, *First Epistle of John*, 8.2.

53. "To say that Augustine exaggerates in speaking against heretics is to say that Augustine tells lies almost everywhere. This is contrary to common knowledge." Luther, *Disputation Against Scholastic Theology*, Thesis 1.

54. "This has already been said. Because men do not know the cross and hate it, they necessarily love the opposite, namely, wisdom, glory, power, and so on. Therefore they become increasingly blinded and hardened by such love, for desire cannot be satisfied by the acquisition of those things which it desires. Just as the love of money grows in proportion to the increase of the money itself, so the dropsy of the soul becomes thirstier the more it drinks, as the poet says: 'The more water they drink, the more they thirst for it.' The same thought is expressed in Eccl 1:8: 'The eye is not satisfied with seeing, nor the ear filled with hearing.' This holds true of all desires. Thus also the desire for knowledge is not satisfied by the acquisition of wisdom but is stimulated that much more. Likewise the desire for glory is not satisfied by the acquisition of glory, nor is the desire to rule satisfied by power and authority, nor is the desire for praise satisfied by praise, and so on, as Christ shows in John 4:13, where he says, 'Every one who drinks of this water will thirst again.' The remedy for curing desire does not lie in satisfying it, but in extinguishing it. In other words, he who wishes to become wise does not seek wisdom by progressing toward it but becomes a fool by retrogressing into seeking 'folly.' Likewise he who wishes to have much power, honor, pleasure, satisfaction in all things must flee rather than seek power, honor, pleasure, and satisfaction in all things. This is the wisdom which is folly to the world." Luther, *Heidelberg*, Proof 22.

discuss these issues further in the concluding chapter). Thus, however, man enters a vicious circle of proud addiction to moral works. In proof 22, Luther describes the mechanism of this addiction. The performance of moral works independently of a theology of the cross produces a love for "wisdom, glory, power, and so on,"[55] namely, an insatiable desire to be recognized as a wise and virtuous person by others. This addiction, like all other addictions, is not cured by feeding the addiction itself, just as addiction to alcohol is not cured by giving more alcohol to the addict. Rather, this spiritual addiction to moralism is cured by a proper evaluation of the cross. The cross of Christ cuts every moralistic claim at the root. Man's will is so bound to sin, his nature so unable to perform virtuous works, and the way of salvation so unparalleled that God had to send and sacrifice his own Son for man's salvation. This is the only way to cure mankind's innate addiction to the glory of moralism.

Luther has very boldly asserted in proof 22 that "he who wishes to become wise does not seek wisdom by progressing toward it but becomes a fool by retrogressing into seeking 'folly' . . . he who wishes to have much power, honor, pleasure, satisfaction in all things must flee rather than seek power, honor, pleasure, and satisfaction in all things. This is the wisdom which is folly to the world."[56] In other words, glory, theoretical and practical wisdom are absent from man's ethical addiction to moral activity and its subsequent high estimation in our eyes and in the eyes of others. Rather, wisdom must be found in "folly," which consists in understanding that man is totally unable to make his own way to the knowledge of the highest good and to ethical enlightenment. This folly consists in realizing that salvation and enlightenment, true ethics and right epistemology, true righteousness and real virtuous life must be found only in the scandalous and foolish cross of Christ. A "cross-less" law considered as an end in itself only produces pride. Whether this law is God's law itself (the Ten Commandments) or an autonomous philosophical law (e.g., Aristotelian's ethics) is not essentially important for Luther.

Augustine draws a similar connection between the abuse of the law and pride. His theology of grace leads him to connect the misapprehension of the law of God and the related overestimation of man's moral activity to the pride that this wrong approach generates. Referring to the Pelagians, the church father writes that they are misled by a wrong concept of justice which binds them to an unrealistic consideration of their own

55. Ivi.
56. Ivi.

ethical constitution and ability: "For they think that, by the strength of their own will, they will fulfill the commands of the law; and wrapped up in their pride, they are not converted to assisting grace. Thus the letter kills (2 Cor 3:6) them either openly, because they are guilty in themselves, by not doing what the law commands; or by thinking that they do it, although they do it not with spiritual love, which is of God. Thus they remain either plainly wicked or deceitfully righteous—manifestly cut off in open unrighteousness, or foolishly elated in fallacious righteousness."[57]

To this, Augustine adds something astonishing for the natural ethical expectation of man's reason. This may be considered the Augustinian version of Luther's "retrogression into seeking folly" principle mentioned earlier: "And by this means—marvellous indeed, but yet true—the righteousness of the law is not fulfilled by the righteousness which is in the law, or by the law, but by that which is in the Spirit of grace."[58] Again, for Augustine the law is not to be considered as a ethical end in itself. The law is truly honored[59] when man realizes that he is not able to honour it, as we have seen in the previous chapters. Thus, man is led to direct his trust both for spiritual salvation and intellectual renewal to the marvelous, paradoxical theology of the cross. Why paradoxical? Not because this truth is paradoxical in itself, as we have seen. Neither Augustine nor Luther teaches this. Rather, it *appears* paradoxical to man, who is addicted to his own ethical expectations and presuppositions which always result in a form of legalistic religion or philosophy. In fact, as Luther adds at the end of proof 22, this wisdom of total dependence on the cross of the incarnated Logos is not folly as such, but "is folly *to the world*."[60]

> 23. The "law brings the wrath" of God (Rom 4:15), kills, reviles, accuses, judges, and condemns everything that is not in Christ.[61]

---

57. Augustine, *Against Two Letters of the Pelagians*, 3.7.20.

58. *Ivi.*

59. It has to be remembered that, for Augustine, the law can never be honored perfectly, but only partially. See the treatment of theses 6–12 of the *Heidelberg Disputation* in chapter 3, and footnote 72 in this chapter.

60. Luther, *Heidelberg*, Proof 22.

61. "Thus Gal 3:13 states, 'Christ redeemed us from the curse of the law;' and: 'For all who rely on works of the law are under the curse' (Gal 3:10); and Rom 4:15: 'For the law brings wrath;' and Rom 7:10: 'The very commandment which promised life proved to be the death of me;' Rom 2:12: 'All who have sinned without the law will also perish without law.' Therefore he who boasts that he is wise and learned in the law boasts in his confusion, his damnation, the wrath of God, in death. As Rom. 2:23 puts it: 'You who boast in the law.'" *Ibid.*, Proof 23.

24. Yet that wisdom is not of itself evil, nor is the law to be evaded; but without the theology of the cross man misuses the best in the worst manner.[62]

In chapter 2 we have already discussed at length the concept expressed in thesis 23. At the same time, we have seen in what way and to what extent Luther bases his idea of the moral law on Augustine, for whom the ethical constitution of mankind's fallennes makes even the most just law of God a means of moral deterioration. The normative role of the law and its relation to man can be properly understood only in a state of enlightening grace: "Let no . . . one, when he has been made to feel ashamed to say that we become righteous through our own selves, without the grace of God working this in us—because he sees, when such an allegation is made, how unable pious believers are to endure it—resort to any subterfuge on this point, by affirming that the reason why we cannot become righteous without the operation of God's grace is this, that He gave the law, He instituted its teaching, He commanded its precepts of good. For there is no doubt that, without His assisting grace, the law is *the letter which kills;*' but when the life-giving spirit is present, the law causes that to be loved as written within, which it once caused to be feared as written without."[63]

Thesis 23 states again the goodness of the law. For Luther, the law of God is a good thing in itself, and also the civil law has its proper importance in its own sphere. The heart of man's ethical problem is not in the things he uses or in the activity of desiring, but in the *use* of these things and in the *direction* of these desires. This is similar to the approach that led Augustine to break with the Aristotelian relegation of passions to the irrational soul, placing them in the rational part of the soul. Thus, the soul will proudly direct its passions toward created things, if the soul is left by itself,

62. "Indeed 'the law is holy' (Rom 7:12), 'every gift of God good' (1 Tim. 4:4), and 'everything that is created exceedingly good,' as in Gen 1:31. But, as stated above, he who has not been brought low, reduced to nothing through the cross and suffering, takes credit for works and wisdom and does not give credit to God. He thus misuses and defiles the gifts of God. He, however, who has emptied himself (cf. Phil 2:7) through suffering no longer does works but knows that God works and does all things in him. For this reason, whether God does works or not, it is all the same to him. He neither boasts if he does good works, nor is he disturbed if God does not do good works through him. He knows that it is sufficient if he suffers and is brought low by the cross in order to be annihilated all the more. It is this that Christ says in John 3:7, 'You must be born anew.' To be born anew, one must consequently first die and then be raised up with the Son of Man. To die, I say, means to feel death at hand." *Ibid.*, Proof 24.

63. Augustine, *The Spirit and the Letter*, 32.19.

while it will direct its passions to the highest good that is God when the soul is led and sustained by that true love that is worked by God himself.[64]

Concerning the central topic of this chapter, i.e., the theology of the cross, Luther, inspired by the Augustinian theology of grace, teaches that to lack an evaluation of the cross always results in a misuse of the law. By preferring a moralistic theology of glory to a totally God-dependent theology of the cross, man "misuses and defiles the gifts of God,"[65] the law of God above everything else. In fact, without the theology of the cross man misuses the best (i.e., the law of God) in the worst manner, that is, by attaching to the law a redeeming and enlightening power that the law does not possess at all. On the one hand, for natural fallen man it is intuitive that a merely practical exercise in virtue generates inner righteousness and moral improvement. On the other hand, it is counterintuitive that this grace-less delight in the law does not increase man in righteousness as God intends it, but rather it hinders him from righteousness. This is because it produces a disordered evaluation of the law itself accompanied by a perverse estimation of man's ethical structures and faculties. Mere knowledge and the autonomous exercise of the law do not produce true righteousness. Rather, as Augustine says, "the knowledge of the law, without the grace of the Spirit, produces all kinds of concupiscence in man."[66]

In thesis 24, Luther talks about "man" in general, which means that the German theologian is addressing mankind as a whole. This is already clear enough from the context of the entire *Heidelberg Disputation*. He is addressing not only a restricted category of people, but Luther is delivering bold anthropological assertions concerning the moral constitution of every man considered as ethically fallen into sin, not as created by God in righteousness. The final thesis of our analysis, however, makes this point even clearer. Even though the first recipients of his message are his colleagues, Luther is not only referring to them, but also to every man considered in light of a Christian anthropology of fallenness.

The condemnation of mankind's abuse of the law is clearly present also in Augustine, as we have already started to see. The bishop states that the law of God, far from being a remedy to man's fallenness, actually arouses his desire to disobey the law itself.[67] This does not mean that for

---

64. Harrison, *Augustine*, 93.

65. Luther, *Heidelberg*, Proof 24.

66. Augustine, *On the Proceedings of Pelagius*, 7.20.

67. "The apostle, wishing to show how hurtful a thing sin is, when grace does not aid us, has not hesitated to say that the strength of sin is that very law by which sin is prohibited. *'The sting of death is sin, and the strength of sin is the law'* (1 Cor 15:56).

man there is no possibility whatsoever of having a proper love of God's law, but "unless divine grace aids us, we cannot love nor delight in true righteousness."[68] Again, this is not the fault of the law, but the problem arises from man's intellectual evaluation and ethical use of this law.[69] Because of his fall into sin, man has lost the creaturely awareness of himself and of everything else.[70] However, this creaturely awareness is indispensable to understand the purpose that God has attached to everything, including his law. Being deprived of this knowledge which includes both intellectual understanding and ethical ability, man is always prone and willing to misuse everything, even his own death, but especially the most holy law of God.[71] Already in his *On Various Questions*, Augustine reached the conclusion that man, because of his fallen ethical state, misuses the law and twists its real purpose: "It [the law] commands what ought to be commanded, and prohibits what ought to be prohibited. 'Was that which is good, then, made death to me? God forbid.' The fault lies in making a bad use of the commandment, which in itself is good. 'The law is good if one uses it lawfully' (1 Tim 1:8). But he makes a bad use of the law who does not subject himself to God in humble piety, so that, with the aid of grace, he may become able to fulfill the law.[72] He who does not use the law

---

Most certainly true; for prohibition increases the desire of illicit action, if righteousness is not so loved that the desire of sin is conquered by that love." Augustine, *The City of God,* 13.5.

68. *Ivi.*

69. "Lest the law should be thought to be an evil, since it is called the strength of sin, the apostle, when treating a similar question in another place, says, '*The law indeed is holy, and the commandment holy, and just, and good. Was then that which is holy made death unto me? God forbid. But sin, that it might appear sin, working death in me by that which is good; that sin by the commandment might become exceeding sinful*' (Rom 7:12–13). *Exceeding,* he says, because the transgression is more heinous when through the increasing lust of sin the law itself also is despised." *Ivi.*

70. Augustine, *Confessions,* 12.15.21; 13.8.9.

71. "As the law is not an evil when it increases the lust of those who sin, so neither is death a good thing when it increases the glory of those who suffer it, since either the former is abandoned wickedly, and makes transgressors, or the latter is embraced, for the truth's sake, and makes martyrs. And thus the law is indeed good, because it is prohibition of sin, and death is evil because it is the wages of sin; but as wicked men make an evil use not only of evil, but also of good things, so the righteous make a good use not only of good, but also of evil things. Whence it comes to pass that the wicked make an ill use of the law, though the law is good; and that the good die well, though death is an evil." Augustine, *The City of God,* 13.5.

72. For Augustine, to "fulfil the law" does not mean to meet *all* its requirements. To fulfil the law means to honor it with the correct attitude of humility and love. See Augustine, *Against Two Letters of the Pelagians,* 3.2.2. Augustine is crystal clear on the

unlawfully receives it to no other end, that his sin, which was latent before the prohibition, should be made apparent by his transgression."[73]

In addition to this diagnosis of man's universal misuse of the law, we may read the same argument in the context of Augustine's criticism of Pelagianism. As we have seen, for Luther the better a created thing is, the more inclined mankind is to misuse that thing. This is true not only concerning creation, but also concerning ethics. We have seen this with the law of God, "the most salutary doctrine of life."[74] It has the most important purpose to direct man to absolute dependency on divine grace. Man, however, makes the law an end in itself, for he misuses it, attaching to it a purpose which is actually the *opposite* of the purpose that God intended. The law has a role in exposing and condemning man, but man's natural intuitive approach to it is that he can actually fulfill it and make himself righteous through moral exercise.

Augustine charges the Pelagians with committing the same error, for he insists that his adversaries make an unlawful extension of the role of the law. This means, first of all, that the Pelagians reach an erroneous conclusion from the very existence of the law: if God gives commands, this necessarily means that man is able to fulfill them.[75] For the African thinker, this objection rhetorically bypasses the reality of man's fallenness, the same reality which the Pelagians claim to consider but which they actually ignore when it comes to dogma. Man *was* able to obey the commandments of the law. However, his willful and conscious fall into sin plunged him into a state of necessity.[76] At the same time, this fall has not lowered God's standard, which is and remains perfection. God's law is still the same and has not changed. What has changed is the *relation* that man has to this law, a change of relation which must be attributed to mankind.

From this follows the Pelagian abuse or bad use of the law. Using the holiness and goodness of God's law and the calling of man to a virtuous

---

impossibility of fulfilling the law understood as a perfect fulfillment of its requirements, with the inevitable imperfection of man's attempt of fulfilling God's law. See *Merits and Remission of Sin, and Infant Baptism*, 2.6.7–7.8; *The Spirit and the Letter*, 36.65; *Against Two Letters of the Pelagians*, 3.7.19. For man's moral perfection considered as possible only after death, see *On the Trinity*, 14.23; *Against Two Letters of the Pelagians*, 3.7.17.

73. Augustine, *On Various Questions*, 1.1.6.

74. Luther, *Heidelberg*, Thesis 1.

75. Augustine treats this objection at length in *On Rebuke and Grace*. See especially *Ibid.*, 2.4; 3.5; 4.6; 6.9.

76. Augustine, *On Man's Perfection in Righteousness*, 4.9.

moral life as pretexts, the Pelagians "praise the law in opposition to grace."[77] Pelagius himself goes so far as to say that the "grace of God" is merely the revelation that God himself gives regarding what man must do in conducting his life. Basically, Pelagius overlaps the meanings of "grace" and "law."[78] Consequently, Pelagius falls into what both Augustine and Luther would define as an abuse of the law. In fact, Pelagius asserts that the will of man is not restored to desire and do the good (that is, first of all, to believe) by God's enlightenment. Rather, the will is restored by man himself.[79] Against the Pelagian abuse of the law of God, Augustine presents a rather strict distinction between "grace" and "law," with their respective definitions. Augustine's language is so straightforward that he almost reaches the definitions of Luther. This clarity it is another proof of the substantial intellectual inspiration that Luther derived from his detailed and extended study of Augustine in his monastic years: "so far are the law and grace from being the same thing, that the law is not only unprofitable, but it is absolutely prejudicial, unless grace assists it; and the utility of the law may be shown by this, that it obliges all whom it proves guilty of transgression to betake themselves to grace for deliverance and help to overcome their evil lusts. For it rather commands than assists; it discovers disease, but does not heal it; nay, the malady that is not healed is rather aggravated by it, so that the cure of grace is more earnestly and anxiously sought for."[80] We cannot stress enough that both Augustine and Luther have nothing against the law of God, or against civil or religious laws, as such. Rather, they oppose the *abuse* of the spiritual law, an abuse that arises when one believes that the law or whatever moral code can make man spiritually enlightened or ethically righteous. The law has the essential goal to *indicate* where righteousness is, but it does not *give* that righteousness.[81] Grace through faith in the cross does, and it is to this faith that the law directs.

77. Augustine, *Against Two Letters of the Pelagians*, 5.10.

78. "He [Pelagius] acknowledges that grace whereby God points out and reveals to us what we are bound to do; but not that whereby He endows and assists us to act." Augustine, *On the Grace of Christ and on Original Sin*, 1.8.9.

79. "[Pelagius] In another passage, after asserting at length that it is not by the help of God, but out of our own selves, that a good will is formed within us." *Ibid*, 1.10.11.

80. *Ibid.*, 1.8.9.

81. "How then manifested without the law, if witnessed by the law? For this very reason the phrase is not, '*manifested without the law*,' but '*the righteousness without the law*,' because it is '*the righteousness of God*;' that is, the righteousness which we have not from the law, but from God—not the righteousness, indeed, which by reason of His commanding it, causes us fear through our knowledge of it; but rather the righteousness which by reason of His bestowing it, is held fast and maintained by us through

THE GLORY AND THE CROSS

We have now concluded the rather lengthy treatment of the theology of Augustine and Luther. As has been already stated, this analysis has been given in order to show the Augustinian foundation of Luther's *Heidelberg Disputation*. Consequently, because the *Heidelberg Disputation* is a manifesto of Luther's thinking, this means that the main aspects of Luther's thought have been proved to have a substantial Augustinian foundation. More specifically, the *Heidelberg Disputation* discusses the issues of free will, the role of the moral normative law with the meaning of virtuous works and life, man's possibility of obtaining righteousness according to the sense of this concept, and the significance of the divine incarnation finalized in the cross of Christ. This distinctively theological treatment has aimed to demonstrate the agreement between Augustine and Luther concerning these topics. Therefore, our analysis has sought to prove the accuracy of the claim that Luther's *Heidelberg Disputation* is Augustinian in nature. It must be remembered that Luther officially and publicly made this claim in front of the General Chapter of the German Augustinian monastic order on April 26, 1518.

However, that was not intended to be the only goal of the current work. In fact, the shared position of Augustine and Luther has relevant philosophical implications. This is evident not only through what the study of Luther's Augustinianism has communicated to us, but also through a comparison of their resulting philosophy of the cross with two of the most representative streams or individuals of the Western philosophy of religion and moral philosophy. In the opinion of the present writer, this comparison will demonstrate a philosophical thesis of Martin Luther, according to which every philosophy of religion advanced on any presuppositional basis other than a full Christology always results in a legalistic position that Luther himself would call 'theology of glory.' More specifically, it is the intention of the author to demonstrate the Pelagian foundation of two of the most famous modern examples of philosophy of religion. Moreover, our treatment will show how, for Luther, this "betrayal" of his Augustinian philosophy of the cross was not an unexpected result, but one known by Luther himself. For this purpose, Leibniz and especially Kant will be taken as representatives of the modern mainstream philosophy of religion. They will be the representatives and the spokespersons of that specific approach to religion which Luther criticizes through Augustine. At the foundations

---

our loving it—'*so that he that glories, let him glory in the Lord*' (1 Cor 1:31)." *Ivi.* See also *Expositions on the Psalms*, 60.10, where Augustine says that the bad use of the law is one of the main sources of scandal and tribulation not only from people who attack Christianity from the outside, but also from those who misuse the law from its inside.

of these two modern thinkers, however, are Aristotle and Pelagius. Both Aristotle and Pelagius, two important characters in the history of the Western world, are the objects of Luther's intellectual antipathy. We have already presented the position of Augustine's greatest adversary, namely, Pelagius. We will now see why it is useful for our analysis to focus on the ethics of Aristotle. Another chapter is necessary in order to prove these claims.

CHAPTER 6

THE ANTITHETICAL CROSS

Are they philosophers? So am I.[1]

THE PREVIOUS CHAPTERS HAVE demonstrated the Augustinian ground of Luther's thought. His position is summarized in his *Heidelberg Disputation*. This analysis does not claim to be complete or comprehensive. However, it is sufficient to show the accuracy of Luther's claim. According to this claim, the theses of his *Heidelberg Disputation* are grounded not only on the authority of Scripture, but also on the teaching of Augustine. We have seen a significant degree of agreement between these two founders of Western culture. The agreement they share pertains to the topics of free will, virtue, righteousness, and the cross. In this sense, they are exponents of the same philosophy of the cross. This strictly theological analysis has interacted only briefly with genuinely philosophical issues. Nevertheless, this parallel between Augustine and Luther will be instrumental for the Lutheran philosophical thesis that this final chapter will discuss.

This final chapter will seek to demonstrate the accuracy of a specific thesis which can be easily deduced from Luther's thought. According to this thesis, every philosophical or theological attempt conducted autonomously from a position of absolute dependence on God is doomed to fall into philosophical moralism and theological legalism. Therefore,

---

1. Luther, *An Open Letter on Translating.*

any theology or philosophy that attempts to ascribe part or all of the work or part or all of the merit of redemption and enlightenment to the autonomous power or will of man is a form of Pelagianism. This means that it does not properly understand the reasons for and the implication of the cross, and it is a "theology of glory." Consequently Luther, through Augustine, presents the theology of the cross as unique and absolutely preeminent, and he rejects any philosophical position that does not start from a proper evaluation of the cross and that does not take into account the logical consequences of the cross.

We may provide a few examples to explain this point. An example taken from theology is the difference between Pelagianism and Semi-Pelagianism. We have already mentioned, albeit briefly, the differences between these two positions.[2] Semi-Pelagianism claims to be a more "God's grace-centered" version of Pelagianism. An example taken from philosophy is the difference between the philosophy of religion of Gottfried Wilhelm von Leibniz and that of Immanuel Kant. As we will see, the former appears to claim that, even though God's aid is very important, man's spontaneous freedom and autonomous virtue are essential; the latter sets forth an entirely autonomous form of religion and ethics in which the idea of God and the concepts of God's grace are only normative concepts to guide mankind to rational enlightenment and to a virtuous life. However, according to Luther's position, the specific differences between the elements of these examples are, in the final analysis, irrelevant. Independently of their specific differences, both Pelagianism and Semi-Pelagianism ascribe a fundamental role to man's neutrally free will and to his autonomous moral effort. The same may be said of the secondary distinctions between Kant and Leibniz. From a Lutheran perspective, they all fall into the category of the theology of glory, inasmuch as they bypass the meaning of the cross. This is because the philosophy of the cross is antithetical to the theology of glory, and vice versa.

---

2. See chapter 2, footnote 2 for an overview of Pelagianism, and footnote 3 for Semi-Pelagianism. We offer another definition which may be helpful in understanding the doctrine of Pelagianism. Moreover, since it is an overarching description, it can be very well adopted as one of the possible portraits of the philosophy of glory opposed by Luther's Augustinian philosophy of the cross here expounded: "Nature, free-will, virtue and law, these—strictly defined and made independent of the notion of God—were the catch-words of Pelagianism: self-acquired virtue is the supreme good which is followed by reward. Religion and morality lie in the sphere of the free spirit; they are won at any moment by man's own effort." von Harnack, *History of Dogma Vol. 5*, chapter 5, paragraph 3.

Luther's concept of the antitheticality of the philosophy of the cross is evident from what he asserts in the *Heidelberg Disputation*, which was previously studied. This idea is clearly visible in theses 19–24, expounded in the previous chapter. Thesis 21 is the clearest example: "A theology of glory calls evil good and good evil. A theology of the cross calls the thing what it actually is."[3] This uncompromising assertion contrasts two radically different approaches. As we have already seen, according to Luther, the theology of glory consists in any theology or philosophy that assigns autonomy to man in the work of redemption and enlightenment. On the one hand, the rejection of the key epistemological principle of the cross leads to ethical errors; on the other hand, mistaken ethics and an erroneous doctrine of the ethical constitution of man lead to the rejection of the key epistemological principle of the cross. According to Luther, if ethics were seen through the epistemological lens of the cross, the result would be a philosophy of the cross in support of a view of man's absolute dependence on God. When a proper understanding of the cross is rejected, a doctrine of the ability of man's will follows, by which he is able to choose neutrally between good and evil. Moreover, man, according to this doctrine, has the spontaneous ability to perform truly virtuous acts, and can reach a state of righteousness by the mere repetition of moral practices. On the contrary, when a proper understanding of the cross is assumed, the coherent conclusions are an acceptance of the necessary bondage of the will, externally received virtue, heteronomous righteousness, and the centrality of the incarnation of the divine Logos. For Luther's Augustinian philosophy of the cross, the cross is the key to both ethics and epistemology, not only theology and general philosophy. The cross throws light on who God is, but also on who man himself is.

Luther's *magnum opus*, *The Bondage of the Will*, offers several sections that clearly allude to the absoluteness of the philosophy of the cross. This is what Luther contends about the issue using strict theological terminology: "nobody is fool enough to doubt that the power and endeavour of 'free-will' is something distinct from faith in Jesus Christ! But Paul denies that anything apart from faith is righteous before God. And if it is not righteous before God, it must be sin; *for with God there remains nothing intermediate between righteousness and sin, that is, as it were, neutral, being neither righteous nor sin.*"[4] With this assertion, we see further that, from a Lutheran perspective, there is no real crucial difference between

---

3. Luther, *Heidelberg*, Thesis 21.
4. Luther, *The Bondage of the Will*, 290. Emphasis added.

Pelagianism and Semi-Pelagianism inasmuch as they belong to the same category. Similarly, there is only a formal difference between the fully man-centered Kantian philosophy of religion and the synergistic theology of Leibniz. Between the philosophy of the cross and the philosophy of glory, whatever form the latter may take, there is no middle ground. For the German thinker, as soon as we attribute to man's will or man's ethics even the slightest autonomy, we are denying the God of the cross, and we are making the atonement unnecessary. In fact, Luther contends that "the guardians of 'free-will' . . . when they assert 'free-will' are denying Christ. For if I obtain the grace of God by my own endeavor, what need have I of the grace of Christ for the receiving of my grace? When I have the grace of God, what do I need besides? . . . So utterly does grace refuse to allow any particle or power of 'free-will' to stand beside it!"[5] Semi-Pelagianism and Plagianism, as well as Leibniz's theology and Kant's philosophy of religion, certainly have a different internal theoretical development. However, they all share the same auto-soteriological[6] conclusions, independently of their formal differences.[7] Accordingly, the philosophy of the cross is diametrically opposed to all four of these approaches.

These assertions about free will are of fundamental importance. We began our analysis of Luther's theses with this very topic. We have justified this approach because, even though the epistemological principle of the cross must lead the entire discussion, it is necessary first to grasp

5. *Ibid.*, 304–305.

6. The meaning of this expression is not difficult to understand. "Soteriological" comes from "soteriology," the branch of systematic theology specifically dedicated to the study of salvation and its related issues. Therefore, "auto-soteriological" refers to a religion or a theology that describes the work of salvation as autonomously accomplished by the recipient of this salvation, that is, man saves himself. This term is common knowledge. I encountered it for the first time in Benjamin B. Warfield, *The Plan of Salvation*, chapter 3. This book was first published in 1915.

7. "A man cannot be thoroughly humbled till he realizes that his salvation is utterly beyond his own powers, counsels, efforts, will and works, and depends absolutely on the will, counsel, pleasure and work of Another—God alone. *As long as he is persuaded that he can make even the smallest contribution to his salvation*, he remains self-confident and does not utterly despair of himself, and so is not humbled before God; but plans out for himself (or at least hopes and longs for) a position, an occasion, a work, which shall bring him final salvation. But he who is out of doubt that his destiny depends entirely on the will of God despairs entirely of himself, chooses nothing for himself, but waits for God to work in him; and such a man is very near to grace for his salvation. So these truths are published for the sake of the elect, that they may be humbled and brought down to nothing, and so saved. The rest of men resist this humiliation; indeed, they condemn the teaching of self-despair; *they want a little something left that they can do for themselves.*" Luther, *The Bondage of the Will*, 100–101. Emphasis added.

clearly Luther's anthropological starting point in order best to understand his view of virtue, righteousness, and the cross itself. Luther confirms this choice in his *The Bondage of the Will*. In fact, the German theologian sees the origin of both theological and philosophical misconceptions in a mistaken notion of man's ethical constitution, a mistake which is centered on the notion of free will. For him, therefore, in order to recover both theology and philosophy, we must start with a discussion about the ethical principle of man's will, being guided by the epistemological principle of the cross:

> It is not irreligious, idle, or superfluous, but in the highest degree wholesome and necessary, for a Christian to know whether or not this will has anything to do in matters pertaining to salvation . . . this is the hinge on which our discussion turns, the crucial issue between us [Luther and Erasmus]; our aim is, simply, to investigate what ability 'free-will' has, in what respect it is the subject of divine action and how it stands related to the grace of God . . . if I am ignorant of the nature, extent and limits of what I can and must do in reference to God, I shall be equally ignorant of the nature, extent and limits of what God can and will do in me . . . If I am ignorant of God's work and power, I am ignorant of God himself; and if I do not know God, I cannot worship, praise, give thanks or serve Him, for I do not know how much I should attribute to myself and how much to him. We need therefore to have in mind a clear distinction between God's power and ours, and God's work and ours . . . Self knowledge, and the knowledge of the glory of God, are bound upon it.[8]

Luther goes on to say that, when we introduce a mistaken notion of the will, the entirety of the philosophy of the cross is fatally damaged. He is again setting forth his thesis according to which apart from a proper understanding of the cross and its related concepts there is only man-centered philosophy and auto-soteriological religion. Of course, his thesis is grounded upon his view of the bondage of the will, according to which God is the only absolutely free power who works on the passive will. This point is central both in *The Bondage of the Will* and in the *Heidelberg Disputation*: ". . . though God, in fact, works all in all (cf. 1 Cor 12.6) . . . all good in us is to be ascribed to God . . . this assertion certainly involves a second, that God's mercy alone works everything, and our will works

8. *Ibid.*, 78.

nothing, but is rather the object of Divine working, else all will not be ascribed to God."[9]

We will see the accuracy of Luther's claim in our study of Kant and Leibniz. While Leibniz holds to a synergistic view of the relation between man and God, Kant asserts a utterly auto-soteriological religion. However, they both start from the presupposition of a neutral freedom of man's will (followed as a consequence by the concepts of virtue, righteousness, and the cross which this view of the will implies). It is true that both of them set forth a certain concept of man's fallenness. Leibniz uses the traditional theological term of "original sin," while Kant coins the expression "radical evil." However, they find the solution to this ethical fault in the virtuous exercise of man's autonomous will. This is why, in spite of the conceptual differences between the two representative authors here chosen, we will see that their final conclusion and their theoretical implications are of the same nature. Both Kant's and Leibniz's philosophy of religion are auto-soteriological. For this reason, it will be shown that their similar conclusions confirm the philosophical thesis of Luther. Thus, the present work will seek to display generally the absolute uniqueness and antitheticality of the philosophy of the cross as opposed to the Pelagian ground of the philosophy of glory, that is, of that philosophy of religion represented by the positions of Kant and Leibniz.

In order to summarize and clarify Luther's claim, we may examine the following diagram in order to understand more deeply what has been stated here. This scheme must be continually borne in mind during the reading of the present chapter. It must be remembered that in the following definitions both the philosophy of the cross and the philosophy of glory are primarily asserted from a divine point of view. This means that the following definitions explain what is God's view of man's will, virtue, righteousness, and the cross.

9. *Ivi.*

	PHILOSOPHY OF THE CROSS (Augustine and Luther)	PHILOSOPHY OF GLORY (E.g.: Pelagianism, Semi-Pelagianism, Scholasticism, Leibniz, Kant)
Will	Morally bound. Man has willfully fallen into necessity willfully to choose evil.	Neutrally free. Auto-determined. Man is able freely to choose between good and evil.
Virtue	Heteronomous. Attainable only by the divine grace of regeneration.	Autonomous. Man is inherently able to perform truly virtuous acts.
Righteousness	External and given. It is the righteousness of Christ, freely given by grace alone through faith alone.	Internal and spontaneous. Reachable through repetitive exercise of moral practices.
Cross	Central. It is the absolutely necessary atoning, expiatory sacrifice to obtain man's redemption and enlightenment.	Complementary. A helpful exemplary aid but not an absolutely necessary atoning, expiatory sacrifice to obtain man's redemption and enlightenment.

I offer a thesis that I plan to develop and defend throughout this final chapter. Like the theses that Luther includes in his *Heidelberg Disputation*, I will also present an introductory proof for the thesis. This introductory proof will be further developed in this same chapter. Moreover, like the text of the *Heidelberg Disputation*, this thesis and its proof, with their commentary, do not claim to be complete and fully satisfactory. Rather, similar to Luther's theses, they are intended to be an intellectual stimulus for further discussion. The present writer hopes that his modest philosophical attempt may be the beginning of an academic discussion on one of the main philosophical theses of Martin Luther that is worth careful consideration, or reconsideration.

> Thesis: *Beyond the philosophy of the cross, there is nothing but Pelagianism.*
>
> Proof: *Beyond an Augustinian philosophy of the cross as expressed by Luther, there is nothing but a form of Pelagianism. This means that when the cross is rejected, what is left is moralism or legalism, Aristotelian ethics or Scholasticism, Kantianism or Leibniz's theodicy, and so on. When God is not the only one at work, man is. If enlightenment and redemption finally depend on the decision of man's will, God is not at the center. If man can autonomously perform virtuous deeds, God is not necessary. If*

*man can spontaneously produce inner righteousness, God is not
essential. If redemption and enlightenment, ethics and epistemology do not start and finish with and through the cross, the cross
is rejected. Thus, man's autonomous morality is praised and the
cross is devalued, or, to use Luther's terminology, philosophers of
glory* "call the good of the cross evil and the evil of a deed good"
*(Proof 21), while Augustine would say that they 'praise the law in
opposition to grace' (Against Two Letters of the Pelagians, 5.10.).
Philosophers of the cross, on the contrary, ascribe all the merit and
work of the regeneration of man to God, inasmuch as* "the friends
of the cross say that the cross is good and works are evil" *(Proof
21), or, to quote Augustine,* "they did not depart from the cross
of Christ, and did not despise Christ's lowliness."[10]

This closing chapter will aim to prove the Lutheran thesis described above.
In order to do that, I will take the philosophy of religion of Leibniz and of
Kant as general representatives of the modern mainstream philosophy of
religion. Thus, the discussion is restricted to Leibniz and Kant and, consequently, to the modern period that they represent. Therefore, the analysis
will not presume to be complete and definitive. However, grounded gen-
eralizations are permissible in philosophy. Moreover, the current analysis
may be the incentive for a further evaluation of the Lutheran thesis which
is discussed here. Thus, the reader may study this specific topic and see
for himself if what is said about Leibniz and Kant is true also for the other
relevant philosophers of the Modern period. The necessary auto-soteriological nature of any deviation from the philosophy of the cross is the first
main thesis out of which two further important Lutheran theses flow.

It is necessary to explain further why the subjects of our analysis
are Leibniz and Kant. This point is essential for the understanding of the
discussion we are seeking to undertake. The reason for such a selection is
grounded, first of all, on the specific condemnation of "human reason"[11]
made by Luther and, secondly, on the two philosophical approaches of the
two thinkers. On the one hand, we have seen that, according to Luther, the
philosophy of glory is the necessary result of that autonomous religious
theorization and practice of man in which he relies only or mainly on his

---

10. Augustine, *The Gospel of John*, 2.3. "Between 'the righteousness of the law,' and
Christian righteousness, there is no mean. He that strayeth from Christian righteous-
ness, must needs fall into the righteousness of the law; that is to say, when he hath lost
Christ, he must fall into the confidence of his own works." Luther, *Commentary on
Galatians*, xvi. "There is no mean betwixt man's work, and the knowledge of Christ."
Ibid., 255.

11. See footnotes 35 and 36 of this chapter.

reason. On the one hand, Leibniz intends to demonstrate the agreement between faith and reason from his rationalistic point of view; while, on the other hand, Kant explicitly asserts that, on matters of religion and theology, pure reason has supremacy. Although following different routes, the entire philosophy of religion of Leibniz and Kant turns on the concept of the objectivity of reason with respect to religion and theology. Therefore, the demonstration that we seek to make here should be clear by now: if the religions of reason of Leibniz and Kant, with their respective peculiar structures, constitute a philosophy of glory, that is, if they offer a theology that shares the same essential contents of Pelagianism or Semi-Pelagianism, this means that the philosophical thesis of Luther, if it is not entirely demonstrated, is at least greatly supported.

In this sense, it must be said that this philosophical analysis is not intended to support a specific theology, nor does it mean to identify which philosophy of religion is the correct one. The following demonstration of this Lutheran thesis does not intend to discriminate between right and wrong philosophy and theology. The present writer has his theological and religious convictions, but this is not the place to discuss them. His convictions are significantly close to most of the thinking of both Augustine and Luther, but also this point will not compromise the demonstration. Using the primary textual sources, the main aim of this chapter is to prove Luther's philosophical thesis, which has been called here the antitheticality of the cross and which has been previously described.

We have already stated that Luther's philosophy of the cross led him to reject theology or philosophy that is not grounded in divine revelation. During the important intellectual development that led Luther to this position, the study of Aristotle played a significant role. It can be argued that Luther's criticism of his contemporary colleagues cannot be sufficiently understood if we ignore Aristotle and the position that Aristotle generally held in the academic world in which Luther worked. More specifically, Aristotle's ethics is the main object of Luther's polemic against Aristotelianism. This means that our analysis cannot exclude a consideration of Luther's evaluation of Aristotle. In fact, according to Luther, the philosophy of glory is influenced by an Aristotelian conception of ethics, where by ethics is intended both normative ethics and ethics in the sense of anthropology, that is, the anthropological constitution of man's nature. Consequently, since the conclusions of Scotist and Occamist Scholasticism were, according to Luther, Pelagian in nature, for the German thinker also Scholasticism was grounded in Aristotle's ethics. Also here, Luther's

Augustinian philosophy of the cross will come to our aid inasmuch as it describes Pelagianism as a wrong approach to ethics with its roots in classical philosophy.

Luther's Criticism of Aristotle's Ethics

Virtually the entire Ethics of Aristotle is the worst enemy of grace.
This is in opposition to the scholastics.[12]

"He who wishes to philosophize by using Aristotle without danger to his soul must first become thoroughly foolish in Christ."[13] This thesis shows that Luther's condemnation of Aristotle should not be understood as a mere academic disagreement with the teaching of the Macedonian philosopher. It is absolutely true, as we shall see, that Luther has several objections to the Stagirite as such. It is also correct to say that Luther believes that Aristotelian misconceptions have implications not only in the restricted academic context, but also for everyday life. However, for Luther, Aristotle is only the tip of the iceberg. In fact, the Lutheran criticism of Aristotelian ethics is the criticism not only of a single individual or of a multifaceted stream of thought. Rather, Luther uses Aristotle as an ideal example of a specific *way* of thinking about ethical issues, and of a general *approach* to ethics. Consequently, Scholasticism, with its continual appeal to Aristotle, is for Luther the main candidate that belongs to this intellectual approach. Also here, Scholasticism must be intended generally, even though Luther was mainly in contact with the Scholastic tradition of Duns Scotus and William of Ockham: "Here Thomas errs in common with his followers with Aristotle who say, 'Practice makes perfect': just as a harp player becomes a good harp player through long practice, so these fools think that the virtues of love, chastity, and humility can be achieved through practice. It is not true."[14]

It is against this ethical approach that Luther focuses most of his anti Aristotelian thinking. As we will see with Leibniz and Kant, this approach

12. Luther, *Disputation Against Scholastic Theology*, Thesis 41.

13. Luther, *Heidelberg*, Thesis 29.

14. Quoted in Althaus, *Luther*, 156. I do not necessarily agree with everything Luther says about Scholastic theologians. As a classical theist, I welcome the developments that thinkers such as Thomas Aquinas and Anselm of Canterbury made in Christian philosophical theology. However, the point here is Luther's emphasis on the Scriptures as the ultimate authority for theology and ethics.

may very well be present also where no claim of belonging to the Aristotelian tradition is made. We start with the topic of free will, proceeding as we have done with the parallel between Augustine and Luther. We will do the same in our analysis of Leibniz and Kant, following the topical pattern that was used in our study of the *Heidelberg Disputation*, namely, free will, virtue, righteousness, and the cross. However, we will not carry out a strictly textual comparison between Aristotle and Luther, as we have done with Augustine and Luther. Rather, we will expound Luther's main points of interest with respect to Aristotelian ethics and their application to theology. This means that we will concentrate on Luther's criticism and opinion of Aristotle, and not on Aristotle as such.

On the foundational topic of free will, Luther believes that the Scholastics are mistaken because, instead of taking a definition of free will from the source that is supposed to be the main authority in Christian theology (i.e., Scripture), they rather presuppose an Aristotelian definition of freedom which they then try to reconcile with the Biblical data. According to them, "from our natural powers we can actually love God above all things."[15] However, with this kind of dogma, "philosophy stinks in our nostrils, as if reason could plead at all times for the best, and we tell tall tales about the law of nature."[16] Of course, the "stink" emanating from the Scholastics comes straight from Aristotle.[17] This conception of the will leads the Scholastics to an erroneous view of sin and, consequently, to a wrong theoretical foundation of the true ethical constitution of man. Also in this case, this error is the result of an improper desire to honor Aristotle: "What, then, is original sin? First, according to the Scholastic theologians, it is the privation or lack of original righteousness. They say that righteousness is only subjectively in the will and so, therefore, also its opposite, the lack of it. This conforms to what Aristotle says in his *Logic* and *Metaphysics* about the category of quality."[18] For Luther, the similarity of this anthropology with the anthropology both of Pelagianism and Semi-Pelagianism is not difficult to perceive. To this ethical position, the German thinker contrasts the view of the apostle Paul.

15. Luther, *Romans*, 217.

16. *Ibid.*, 18.

17. "We praise the rational principle of the continent man and of the incontinent, and the part of their soul that has such a principle, since it urges them aright and towards the best objects." Aristotle, *Nicomachean Ethics*, 1.13, 1102b 15.

18. Luther, *Romans*, 167.

> Second, but according to the apostle and in accordance with an
> understanding that is marked by the simplicity of Christ Jesus,
> it [original sin] is not merely the privation of quality in the will,
> indeed, not merely the loss of light in the intellect or of the
> strength in the memory, but, in a word, the loss of all upright-
> ness and of the power of all our faculties of body and soul and
> of the whole inner and outer man. Over and beyond this, it is
> the proneness toward evil; the loathing of the good; the disdain
> for light and wisdom but fondness for error and darkness; the
> avoidance and contempt of good works but an eagerness for do-
> ing evil.[19]

It follows that Scholasticism, guided by Aristotle's ethics, has also a non-
Pauline view of virtue. We have come now to the second topic. Luther
makes a strict connection between the erroneous doctrines of free will and
sin, and a misleading concept of virtue and virtuous practice. The latter
is the consequence of the former: "Either I have never understood the
matter or the Scholastics did not deal adequately with sin and grace. For
they imagine that original sin, just like actual sin, is entirely taken away, as
if sin is something that could be moved in the flick of an eyelash, as darkness is by light. The ancient holy fathers Augustine and Ambrose, however,
deal with these issues quite differently, namely, according to the method of
Scripture. But the scholastics follow the method of Aristotle in his *Ethics*,
and he bases sinfulness and righteousness and likewise the extent of their
actualization on what a person does."[20] Here Luther explicitly asserts that
the theological misconceptions of Scholasticism are grounded in its inner
Aristotelianism, especially in its presupposed Aristotelian ethics. Nevertheless, for Luther revealed divine ethics and human autonomous ethics
are antithetical to each other. In fact, "it is wrong to define virtue in the
way of Aristotle.[21] It makes us perfect and produces laudable acts only in
the sense that it makes us perfect and it causes our acts to be praiseworthy
before man and before our own eyes. Before God this is abominable, and
the opposite would please him much more."[22]

Consequently, a misleading concept of righteousness is what follows.
However, before treating this issue, it must again be underlined that the
German theologian considers Aristotle as the highest representative of
that general approach to ethics which is the most intuitive for humanity's

19. *Ivi.*

20. *Ibid.*, 128.

21. Cf., *Nicomachean Ethics*, 1.12–13.

22. Luther, *Romans*, 266.

fallen nature. Aristotle is not merely an academic adversary. For Luther, Aristotle's ethics constitutes the ideal, archetypal representative of the ethical position that is most natural, spontaneous, and intuitive for mankind considered in his fallenness. However, for Luther, something that is natural, spontaneous, and intuitive is not necessarily correct or true. A thief may find the act of stealing absolutely natural, spontaneous, and intuitive, but this perception does not render his crime acceptable. The following is Luther's assertion regarding man's natural ethics: "Human teachings reveal the righteousness of man, i.e., they teach who is righteous and how man can be and become righteous before himself and his fellow men. But only the gospel reveals the righteousness of God (i.e., who is righteous and how man can be and become righteous before God) by that faith alone by which one believes the word of God."[23] More importantly, Luther's words regarding Aristotle as the highest exponent of man's natural ethics deserve particular attention. The German thinker does not explicitly state what has been asserted regarding the representative role that the Stagirite would play. However, Luther is contrasting two opposing views of righteousness: righteousness according to "human teachings," and righteousness according to divine revelation. As representative of the former, Luther quotes Aristotle. This is the reason why I think it is accurate to say that for Luther Aristotle is the ideal example of that secular ethics which is most natural for man considered as fallen and that, therefore, is independent of divine revelation.

> The righteousness of God must be distinguished from the righteousness of man which comes from works—as Aristotle in the third chapter of his *Ethics* clearly indicates. According to him, righteousness follows upon and flows from actions. But, according to God, righteousness precedes works and works result from it.[24]

It is interesting to point out that, while Luther refers to Aristotle as the representative of man's natural ethics, he also refers to Augustine as the representative of divinely revealed ethics. In fact, in the same passage he quotes *The Spirit and the Letter*: "It is called the righteousness of God, because by His bestowal of it He makes us righteous, just as we read that salvation is the Lord's, because He makes us safe."[25] The German thinker is contrasting Aristotle and Augustine. This is consistent both with Lu-

23. *Ibid.*, 17–18.

24. *Ibid.*, 18.

25. Augustine, *The Spirit and the Letter*, 11.18.

ther's teaching and with his effort to substitute the study of Aristotle and Scholasticism with the study of Augustine and Scripture. We have already discussed and demonstrated the agreement between Luther and Augustine in the previous chapters. It follows that for Luther it is permissible to quote Augustine as an authority against the Aristotelianism advocated by his Scholastic adversaries. Both for Augustine and Luther, the righteousness of man is the antithesis of the righteousness of God.

We can now summarize our findings so far. Aristotle has a realist, autonomous view of virtue and righteousness, while Luther has a legal, heteronomous view. Aristotle claims that repeated deeds of virtue are the source and the cause of the quality of virtue in man. In contrast, Luther asserts that "the fruit does not produce the tree, but the tree the fruit. Works and actions do not produce virtue, as Aristotle claims,[26] but virtue determines action, as Christ teaches. For a second act presupposes the first one, and the prerequisite of an action is substance and power just as there is no effect without a cause."[27] Moreover, Aristotle states that righteousness is a quality of the soul acquired through virtuous moral practice. Now, Luther clearly teaches that a man can actually improve in virtue. The German thinker would identify this process with the theological term of sanctification. However, the righteousness received in justification, even though it is not separated, is still distinct from the virtue received in the process of sanctification. For Luther, a justified righteous man always becomes virtuous. Justification and sanctification, however, are two different things. Justification is a mere *legal* external declaration of innocence, while sanctification is a *factual* modification of man's mind. For the theologian of Wittenberg, one of the main errors of those who apply Aristotelian categories to theology and philosophy is exactly to confuse these two things, that is, to overlap justification and sanctification: "The Scripture interprets 'righteousness' and 'unrighteousness' quite differently from the way in which the philosophers and the jurists do. This is shown by the fact that they consider them as qualities of the soul. But, in the Scriptures, righteousness depends more on the reckoning of God than on the essence of the thing itself."[28] It seems clear that at the very basis of these two ethical approaches, there are two different concepts of righteousness. In fact, for Aristotelianism, and more seriously for Scholasticism, righteousness is defined according to human philosophical criteria and so applied to divine

---

26. Aristotle, *Nicomachean Ethics*, 3.7.1114a 4–7. See also *Ibid.*, 3.7.1113b 4–10.

27. Luther, *Romans*, 228.

28. Luther, *Romans*, 141.

things. On the contrary, Luther asserts that the definition of righteousness must be derived from divinely revealed criteria and so applied to human things: "For a person that possesses only the quality of righteousness does not have righteousness, for he is an unrighteous sinner through and through, but that person has righteousness whom God mercifully reckons as righteous because he confesses his unrighteousness and implores the divine righteousness; it is such a man that God wants to regard as righteous. Thus we are all born in iniquity, i.e., unrighteousness, and we die in it, but we are righteous, through faith in God's word, only as he mercifully regards us as righteous."[29] From a Lutheran perspective, the Aristotelian and Scholastic epistemological cycle is therefore horizontal: it starts with man, it goes through man and ends with man.[30] The epistemological cycle

---

29. *Ivi.*

30. Luther's report of Aristotelian ethics, although mediated by Scholasticism, is generally accurate. "Virtue, then, being of two kinds, intellectual and moral, intellectual virtue in the main owes both its birth and its growth to teaching (for which reason it requires experience and time), while moral virtue comes about as a result of habit, whence also its name (*ethike*) is one that is formed by a slight variation from the word *ethos* (habit). From this it is also plain that none of the moral virtues arise in us by nature; for nothing that exists by nature can form a habit contrary to its nature. For instance the stone which by nature moves downwards cannot be habituated to move upwards, not even if one tries to train it by throwing it up ten thousand times; nor can fire be habituated to move downwards, nor can anything else that by nature behaves in one way be trained to behave in another. *Neither by nature, then, nor contrary to nature do the virtues arise in us; rather we are adapted by nature to receive them, and are made perfect by habit.* Again, of all the things that come to us by nature we first acquire the potentiality and later exhibit the activity (this is plain in the case of the senses; for it was not by often seeing or often hearing that we got these senses, but on the contrary we had them before we used them, and did not come to have them by using them); but *the virtues we get by first exercising them*, as also happens in the case of the arts as well. For the things we have to learn before we can do them, we learn by doing them, e.g. men become builders by building and lyreplayers by playing the lyre; so too *we become just by doing just acts*, temperate by doing temperate acts, brave by doing brave acts." *Nicomachean Ethics*, 2.1103a, emphasis added. See also *Ibid.*, 3.111121a1–3. Even though Aristotle says that "none of the moral virtues arise in us by nature," he also asserts that "we are adapted by nature to receive them, and are made perfect by habit," that is, man has a natural predisposition to virtues and righteousness, at least partially: "All men think that each type of character belongs to its possessors in some sense by nature; for from the very moment of birth we are just or fitted for self control or brave or have the other moral qualities; but yet we seek something else as that which is good in the strict sense—we seek for the presence of such qualities in another way. For both children and brutes have the natural dispositions to these qualities, but without reason these are evidently hurtful." *Ibid.*, 6.1144b4–4. Moreover, in utter opposition to Luther's convictions, Aristotle also claims the essential importance of a good education for virtues and righteousness: "Thus, in one word, states of character arise out of like activities. This is why the activities we exhibit must be of a certain kind; it is because the states

of the philosophy of the cross, however, is vertical inasmuch as it starts with God, it goes through man, and it finishes with God.

We face now the final point, the cross. For Luther, if Aristotelian ethics is coherently assumed, the cross is denied. We have already mentioned more than once Luther's *Disputation Against Scholastic Theology*. In this document, Luther explicitly asserts his uncompromising rejection of Aristotelian ethics, as well as every attempt to theologize and philosophize according to Aristotelian categories and presuppositions. This disputation took place the year before the *Heidelberg Disputation*. On the occasion of the baccalaureate of one of Luther's students, Franz Günther, the German theologian produced a set of ninety-seven theses directed against Scholasticism and Aristotelianism, which were intended to be the beginning of a discussion that took place on September 4, 1517. Let us quote only a few of the 97 theses that constitute that document.

> *41. Virtually the entire Ethics of Aristotle is the worst enemy of grace. This is in opposition to the scholastics.*
>
> *43. It is an error to say that no man can become a theologian without Aristotle. This is in opposition to common opinion.*
>
> *44. Indeed, no one can become a theologian unless he becomes one without Aristotle.*
>
> *50. Briefly, the whole Aristotle is to theology as darkness is to light. This is in opposition to the scholastics.*[31]

These are only some of the theses of this disputation from which we may demonstrate Luther's criticism of Aristotle. We see how Luther places the Christian conception of grace with its resultant ethics and the Aristotelian ethics in diametrical opposition. For Luther, such an Aristotelian background of theology and philosophy destroys the message of the philosophy of the cross. The supernatural regenerating and enlightening power that flows out of the cross becomes merely "useful, to be sure, but not necessary, and then also we do not carry a defect in our nature because of

---

of character correspond to the differences between these. It makes no small difference, then, whether we form habits of one kind or of another from our very youth; it makes a very great difference, or rather all the difference." *Ibid.*, 2.1103b21–25. Luther has always believed in the importance of a good education, both academically and morally, and for people of every rank. What he opposes is the claim that mere education, whatever form it may assume, is able to give righteousness as God intends it. At its best, education may bring forth a civil, external righteousness, not a spiritual, internal one.

31. Luther, *Disputation Against Scholastic Theology*, Theses 41, 43, 45, 50.

the sin of Adam but are sound in our natural power."[32] As we have seen, the cross of the incarnate Logos is the atoning sacrifice that makes man's redemption and enlightenment possible. On the one hand, the philosophy of the cross, having the cross as its epistemological and ethical source, points to man's fallen will, to his utter self-centeredness that hinders him in achieving virtue, and to his lack of divinely intended righteousness; on the other hand, the Aristotelianism of Scholasticism interprets the cross according to human categories and, therefore, it results in the teaching of the autonomy of man's will and moral activity. This means that, for Luther, Aristotelian ethical presuppositions in philosophy and theology rule out the cross, which is the central epistemological axiom that allows man to know God and his ethical demands, as well as man himself and his ethical nature. This Lutheran analysis of the ethics of Aristotle was already clear *in nuce* in our study of the Augustinian basis of the *Heidelberg Disputation*, in particular thesis 25. We possess now all the elements to understand this thesis even further. It may very well be used as a succinct summary of Luther's criticism of Aristotelian Scholasticism.

> 25. He is not righteous who does much, but he who, without work, believes much in Christ.
>
> Proof. For the righteousness of God is not acquired by means of acts frequently repeated, as Aristotle taught, but it is imparted by faith, for "He who through faith is righteous shall live" (Rom 1:17), and "Man believes with his heart and so is justified" (Rom 10:10). Therefore I wish to have the words "without work" understood in the following manner: Not that the righteous person does nothing, but that his works do not make him righteous, rather that his righteousness creates works. For grace and faith are infused without our works. After they have been imparted the works follow. Thus Rom 3:20 states, "No human being will be justified in His sight by works of the law," and, "For we hold that man is justified by faith apart from works of law" (Rom 3:28). In other words, works contribute nothing to justification.[33]

Now, how do we turn our attention from Aristotle to Leibniz and Kant? From a Lutheran point of view, what is the common philosophical fault that connects Aristotle and Scholasticism with the philosophers whom we shall now discuss? It consists in applying human definitions to divine things instead of applying divine definitions to human things. Expressed

---

32. Luther, *Romans*, 218.

33. Luther, *Heidelberg*, Thesis 25.

in other words, this error consists in interpreting divine things according to human definitions, instead of interpreting human things according to divine definitions. In the following passage, Luther's words are directed towards Erasmus. Notwithstanding, they can be also applied to the Scholastics of his day. Even though Luther is discussing primarily God's decree of predestination, the same concept may be applied to our current discussion: 'This is what offended so many men of outstanding ability, men who have won acceptance down so many ages. At this point, they demand that God should act according to man's idea of right, and do what seems proper to themselves—or else that He should cease to be God! . . . Flesh does not deign to give God glory to the extent of believing Him to be just and good when He speaks and acts above and beyond the definitions of Justinian's Code, or the first book of Aristotle's Ethics!"[34] As we have said, the final result of this foundational hermeneutical mistake is a doctrine of neutral free will, autonomous virtue, and self-produced righteousness, with the related denial of the absolute necessity of the cross or the restriction of its sphere of influence and power. In Luther's view, Aristotle is the philosophical father of this approach, Pelagians are his theological sons, and Scholasticism is the most recent heir of his age.

The question we now ask ourselves is this: do we find the same Aristotelian ethical approach of Scholasticism in Leibniz and Kant? We have said that Luther maintains that Pelagianism is grounded in Aristotelian ethics, and not the opposite, for evident chronological and structural reasons. Therefore, we will now examine whether the philosophies of religion of Leibniz and Kant are Pelagian in nature. Do these men also come to the same Pelagian conclusion of the philosophy of glory previously outlined? Do Leibniz and Kant, with their continual appeal to reason and rationality, confirm Luther's claim according to which every theology that places reason as the judge of revelation necessarily results in Pelagianism? After all, Aristotle and Scholasticism were born prior to Luther, and it is not impossible to make predictions on things which have already happened. But do we find Luther's philosophical thesis to be accurate, and his prediction to be correct, also with respect to Leibniz and Kant, who lived after Luther's death? We will now attempt to demonstrate, through the aforementioned modern philosophers, the accuracy of Luther's claim. Both Leibniz and Kant, in different ways and using different terms, arrive at similar conclusions of the philosophy of glory previously described. Since they do not coherently presuppose divine revelation, personified

34. Luther, *The Bondage of the Will*, 232–233.

in the cross, the independent logical theorizations[35] described by Leibniz and the autonomous rationalizing[36] illustrated by Kant necessarily fall into the philosophy of glory. The former is represented by Leibniz's attempt to resolve theological issues in his *Theodicy*, while the latter is represented by Kant's philosophy of religion of pure reason in his *Religion Within the Boundaries of Mere Reason*.

We start with the philosopher of Königsberg. We will see that Kant's exposition of the religion of reason is consistently Pelagian. This very reason alone is significant evidence in favor of Luther's claim according

35. "Reason, by her inferences and syllogism, explains the pulls of the Scripture of God whichever way she likes . . . all her gabblings are stupid and absurd, and especially so when she begins to make a show of her wisdom in holy things . . . she bases her judgment of things and words that are of God upon the customs and concerns of men; and what is more perverse than that, when the former are heavenly and the latter earthly? Thus in her stupidity she betrays herself as thinking of God only as of man." Luther, *The Bondage of the Will*, 152. Some clarifications are here necessary. Luther is not condemning reason *as such*, nor he is despising logical thinking. Luther's focus is on that use of speculative reason that proceeds independently of divine revelation. This is what Mario Miegge says: "Luther has no confidence in speculative reason (*Vernunft*). This is in harmony with his nominalist presuppositions. He does not spare the most bitter and irreverent invectives against 'human reason' as a source of metaphysical knowledge. However, Luther does not intend to replace reason with a sort of 'irrationalism': reason as 'intellect,' intended as the logical ability to be exercised upon the data of empirical experience or of divine revelation, is fully acknowledged . . . In the occasion of the dramatic and solemn Diet of Worms, Luther himself asked to be disproved 'by Scripture or by clear reason,' *Scriptura aut ratione*. This binomial is not incompatible with the strong emphasis that Luther consistently places on 'Scripture alone,' as the foundation of Christian dogma. The '*ratio*' that he sustains is intended as an honest and convincing logic applied to the interpretation of Scripture. It is not *Vernunft* applied to metaphysics: rather, it is the humble *Verstand* at the necessary service of the Christian truth. A believing reason, *glaubiger Verstand*, an intelligence embodied with faith, inspired by faith, and that explicates itself in the sphere of faith. Luther commits the reformation of the church to this believing faith, which is nourished by the living core of the Holy Scripture, and guided by the intimate knowledge of that Gospel that is the center of the Scripture." Miegge, *Lutero*, 338. The translation from Italian to English is mine. Luther, therefore, does not condemn the logical use of reason as such, but his condemnation is directed towards philosophers and theologians who hide their attempts to defend their ethical presuppositions under the clothes of supposed rational objectivity. This has to be kept in mind every time Luther mentions the word "reason."

36. "The metaphysical theologians deal with a silly and crazy fiction when they dispute about the question whether there can be opposite appetites in one and the same subject, and when they invent the notion of the spirit, i.e. reason, is something absolute or separate by itself and in its own kind an integral whole and that, similarly, opposite to it also sensuality, or the flesh, constitutes equally an integral whole. These stupid imaginations cause them to lose sight of the fact that the flesh is a basic weakness or wound of the whole man which grace has only begun to heal in his reason or spirit." Luther, *Romans*, 213. In the same passage, Luther quotes Augustine, *Against Julian*, 2.5.12.

to which the religion of man's autonomous reason always ends in a form of Pelagianism. We now focus our study on the text of *Religion Within the Boundaries of Mere Reason* and on the philosophy of glory contained therein.

Kant's Philosophy of Religion

Pelagius sang the same tune long ago, when he assigned to "free-will" not desire nor endeavor only, but complete power to do and fulfill all things.[37]

The aim of this analysis is not to give a Lutheran confutation or answer to the philosophy of religion of Kant set forth in his *Religion Within the Boundaries of Mere Reason*. Rather, the present work will show how Kant's discovery of the religion of pure reason is not his own discovery, but Luther's. With this I mean that, as the aforementioned quotes adequately demonstrates, Luther foresaw that a religion developed through the autonomous theorizing of reason and independently of revelation necessarily results in Kant's religion, that is, in Pelagianism, a technical term which I use deliberately. In fact, we will see that Kant's philosophy of religion, with his teaching of liberty, virtue, righteousness, and salvation, consists in a systematic reinterpretation of Pelagian theology with transcendental terminology. Therefore, the essence of the religion developed by Kant was nothing particularly new in the history of Western philosophy. Independently of the original philosophical nature that Kant intended to give to his philosophy of religion, its similarities with Pelagian theology will clearly emerge.

Considering the nature of the present work, there is no time to give a detailed exposition of Kant's philosophy in general and of his approach to religion in particular. This will rather be taken for granted in the knowledge of the reader. For our current purpose, it is enough to summarize briefly the intention of Kant. Kant intends to interpret religion, and especially the revealed religion of Christianity, in light of the morality of pure reason. This is because in the relation between faith and reason (as Kant intends and places them), reason has a criteriological primacy. His position can be summarized in this citation from *The Conflict of the Faculties*: "Reason alone is the source of the universality, unity, and necessity in the

37. Luther, *The Bondage of the Will*, 167.

tenets of faith that are the essence of any religion as such, which consists in the morally practical (in what we ought to do)."[38]

As is to be expected, Kant starts his book with a discussion of human nature and its related will. After the two prefaces, Kant redefines the concept of "human nature." For him, the nature of man is not a fixed anthropological constitution that places man in a state of moral necessity, as the traditional Christian definition of human nature supposes. Rather, the nature of man is merely the foundational subjective use of liberty which is prior to and at the basis of all perceivable acts.[39] Since the first chapter of *Religion* is dedicated to the problem of evil, Kant also adds that the foundation of evil that man commits cannot lie in any prior determination of nature, whatever it may be. Evil acts flow only out of the free auto-determination of the liberty, that is, only in a maxim that freedom presents to itself and subsequently accepts. Only in this sense, can a man be called evil.[40] Kant seems to be aware of the objection according to which placing the origin of evil (or good) acts in an original determination of the will would generate an *in infinitum* quest going back in search of this foundational determination. To this objection, Kant does not give any real answer. He resolves this fundamental inconsistency by calling this primordial determination "inscrutable."[41]

38. Immanuel Kant, *Conflict of the Faculties*, 17.

39. "By the nature of man we here mean only that subjective ground of the use of his freedom precedent to any act falling under sense let this ground be what it may. Farther, this subjective ground must be figured to be an act of freedom; for if otherwise, neither the use nor abuse made by man of his free choice could be imputed to him as his deed; and his indwelling good or evil would not be moral." Kant, *Religion*, Book 1, Exordium, 19–20.

40. "The ground of moral evil can lie in no object determinative of the will through the intervention of an appetite; neither can it lie in any physical instinct, but only in a rule, i.e. in a maxim self-appointed by choice to its own freedom. But what now may be the subjective ground of adopting such a maxim, and discarding its contrary, is an ulterior question, that cannot be resolved. For were this last ground, concerning which question is made, no longer a general maxim, but a mere physical determination, then would the use of our freedom be explicable upon mere natural causes, which, however, is repugnant to the very idea of a supersensible causality. When, therefore, it is said, 'Mankind is by Nature Good,' or 'He is by Nature Evil,' those positions merely mean 'he contains within him an unsearchable last ground of adopting good or of adopting bad maxims;' which ground, unfathomable even by his own reason, pervades and tinges so universally the species, as to serve for an exponent whereby to indicate the character of the whole race." *Ibid.*, 20.

41. "That the last subjective ground of adopting moral maxims must be inscrutable (*by man*) is already self-evident from this consideration, viz. that since their appointment is FREE, the ground of such a choice can not be sought in any physical spring. It can lie only in a maxim. Now, since this maxim must have its ground, and since out

Man, therefore, has for Kant the ability freely to determine whether he is evil or good, according to the kind of maxims the will determines to accept: "the freedom of the will is endowed with this peculiar property, that it never can be determined by any spring to any act, except in so far as mankind has himself adopted, and taken up that spring into his maxim, i.e., has transformed it into a universal rule, according to which he wills to conduct himself. In no other manner can a spring, be it what it may, consist with the absolute spontaneity of a free choice."[42] "Absolute spontaneity" means also absolute liberty and autonomy from any necessity. In fact, even though Kant recognizes a kind of primordial inclination of mankind to evil which somehow corrupts this neutrality of the will,[43] he also says that man is able to direct his liberty to the proper order of the maxims. Furthermore, this correction has nothing to do with supernatural regeneration or enlightenment, but it is rather a mere autonomous re-education. Of course, this concept is grounded in the Kantian conviction according to which the moral law tells man not only what he must do, but it informs man also what he is able to do.[44] In this sense, the law is all that

---

of and beyond maxims no determinatives of free choice can be assigned, it is manifest that we may recede backwards *in infinitum* along this subjective chain, without ever arriving at the last link, *i.e.* without ever fathoming a maxim's absolutely last ground." *Ibid.*, footnote.

42. Kant, *Religion*, Explanatory Scholion, 23–24.

43. ". . . mankind is only evil so far forth as he inverts the ethical order of those springs which he adopts into his maxims . . . If, now, there be in human nature a proneness to this inverting of the proper order of the will's springs, then is there in man a natural bias toward evil; and such bias is itself morally evil, for it must be regarded as seated in the will's free causality, and consequently as imputable. This evil is radical, for it corrupts man's maxims in their last ground. Moreover, as a natural bias, it never can be extirpated by any exertions of the human subject, for this could only take place by force of good maxims, which, when the supreme subjective ground of all maxims is already corrupt, never can occur; nevertheless it can be outweighed, being met with in mankind who are free agents." *Ibid.*, Book 1, Section 3, 41–42.

44. "If man is depraved at the bottom of his heart, how is it possible that he, by his own strength, can bring about this revolution within, and become, of his own accord, a good man? Nevertheless, duty thus enjoins; but the law ordains nothing impracticable, wherefore we must hold that the revolving takes place in the cast of thinking; and that the gradual reform affects the bent of the sensory so far forth as this last throws obstacles before the first: that is to say, when by one single inflexible determination, mankind retroverts his will's perverted bias for choosing evil maxims, he then puts on a new man, and becomes, in regard of his principles and inward-mindedness, placed in a capacity for good: while, perceptibly, it is only through a long track of conduct that he can be seen even by himself to have grown into a good man. In a single word, it is to be hoped, that this purity of principle, now chosen as his dominant rule of life, will suffice to keep him unswervingly steady, along the good though narrow rail way of a perpetual progression from bad to better." *Ibid.*, Book 1, Section 4, General Scholion, 56.

man's liberty needs in order to lead him both to morality and to religion: "ethics issues inevitably in religion."[45]

This Kantian philosophy of liberty applied to religion has its roots in Pelagianism. The Augustinian philosophy of the cross of Luther asserts that man's natural religion of reason is Pelagianism. Kant, on the issue of liberty, has confirmed this assertion. Pelagius also believed that the will is in a state of neutrality with respect to choosing between good and evil, that is, between obedience to God's commandments and disobedience.[46] This is because for both Pelagius and Kant, although using different terms and following different intellectual roads, sin is not an ethical fallenness which corrupts the very nature of man including his reason and will. Rather, the concept of "sin" is mainly a matter of disordered legality, that is, sin is merely a "bad example" which generates "bad habits," and evil in the world is present because men have followed the bad example. Of course, the worst example is the primordial one of Adam, the only one who, Pelagians seem to imply, has been perverted in his inner nature by the fall into sinfulness.[47] The will, therefore, has only been wrongly di-

45. *Ibid*, First Preface 9, 4. Or course, this law is self-given by reason through the acceptance of the autonomous will. It is not an heteronomous law a priori accepted by man's will. Even though there is nothing wrong in an heteronomous law as such, it has always to be under the critique of practical reason.

46. "They, however, must be resisted with the utmost ardor and vigor who suppose that without God's help, the mere power of the human will in itself, can either perfect righteousness, or advance steadily towards it; and when they begin to be hard pressed about their presumption in asserting that this result can be reached without the divine assistance, they check themselves, and do not venture to utter such an opinion, because they see how impious and insufferable it is. But they allege that such attainments are not made without God's help on this account, namely, because God both created man with the free choice of his will, and, by giving him commandments, teaches him, Himself, how man ought to live; and indeed assists him, in that He takes away his ignorance by instructing him in the knowledge of what he ought to avoid and to desire in his actions: and thus, by means of the free-will naturally implanted within him, he enters on the way which is pointed out to him, and by persevering in a just and pious course of life, deserves to attain to the blessedness of eternal life." Augustine, *The Spirit and the Letter*, 2.4.

47. "No doubt all they imitate Adam who by disobedience transgress the commandment of God; but he is one thing as an example to those who sin because they choose; and another thing as the progenitor of all who are born with sin. All His saints, also, imitate Christ in the pursuit of righteousness; whence the same apostle, whom we have already quoted, says: '*Be imitators of me, as I am also of Christ*' (1 Cor 11:1). But besides this imitation, His grace works within us our illumination and justification, by that operation concerning which the same preacher of His [name] says: '*Neither is he that plants anything, nor he that waters, but God that gives the increase*' (1 Cor 3:7) . . . As therefore He, in whom all are made alive, besides offering Himself as an example of righteousness to those who imitate Him, gives also to those who believe in Him the

rected, not structurally damaged or corrupted, or at least not so seriously
as to plunge man into a state of moral necessity.

Of course, it is intuitive that the Kantian doctrine of liberty results in
man's full ability to avoid sin without any enlightening supernatural aid.
This is due to the fact that Kant seems to retain the term "sin" only to give a
shape of Christianity to his philosophy of religion. "Sin," for Kant is merely
the wrong determination of the will in accepting maxims which are not
contemplated by his practical reason. It is interesting to see how also Ce-
lestius, a leading figure of the Pelagian party, makes an appeal to reason
in order to support his view of the will as able autonomously to avoid sin.

> *"First of all,"* says he, *"he must be asked who denies man's ability
> to live without sin, what every sort of sin is—is it such as can be
> avoided? Or is it unavoidable? If it is unavoidable, then it is not
> sin; if it can be avoided, then a man can live without the sin which
> can be avoided. No reason or justice permits us to designate as
> sin what cannot in any way be avoided."* Our answer to this is,
> that sin can be avoided, if our corrupted nature be healed by
> God's grace, through our Lord Jesus Christ. For, in so far as it is
> not sound, in so far does it either through blindness fail to see,
> or through weakness fail to accomplish, that which it ought to
> do; *"for the flesh lusts against the spirit, and the spirit against the
> flesh"* (Gal 5:17) so that a man does not do the things which he
> would.[48]

As we said, for Kant, if there is a law, there is ability. Consequently, man is
able to keep the law and to meet the requirements of this law. Also here, no
supernatural help is necessary; on the contrary, according to Kant external
help would lead man to moral laziness. For Kant, grace and law mean the
same thing, and grace is merely the efficacious knowledge of the practical
law that conducts to salvation (which, we remember, is a mere re-education
of the will). Both Augustine and Luther, as well as Kant and Pelagius, agree
that a good will is a will that finds delight in the law. This finding delight,
however, is defined by these two groups in two radically different ways.
We have already discussed the agreement between Augustine and Luther.

---

hidden grace of His Spirit, which He secretly infuses even into infants; so likewise he, in
whom all die, besides being an example for imitation to those who willfully transgress
the commandment of the Lord, depraved also in his own person all who come of his
stock by the hidden corruption of his own carnal concupiscence. It is entirely on this
account, and for no other reason, that the apostle says: 'By one man sin entered into
the world, and death by sin, and so passed upon all men; in which all have sinned' (Rom
5:12)." Augustine, *Merits and Remission of Sin, and Infant Baptism*, 1.9.10.

48. Augustine, *On Man's Perfection in Righteousness*, 1.2.

Here we are interested in the agreement between Kant and Pelagianism inasmuch as we wish to demonstrate Luther's philosophical thesis regarding the antithetical nature of the cross. Even here, the similarity between Pelagianism and Kantianism is remarkable. There are several Augustinian passages that describe the Pelagian position and where the similarities of this theology to Kant's religion of the will are evident.

In light of such doctrine of the absolute freedom of the will, it is necessary that Kant would include in his treatise on religion also his view of virtue. Kant very clearly teaches that we make ourselves virtuous. More precisely, we make ourselves worthy of God's favor. Moreover, this divine approval is not restrained in a specific sphere of revelation. In fact, revealed knowledge is not necessary to be virtuous in the eyes of the divinity. Only a properly intended and practiced moral life is the indispensable requirement.[49] Now, it is true that Pelagianism gives more importance to the presence of a personal divinity. However, Pelagianism and Kantianism have an approach to virtue that is very similar at its foundation. They both deeply undermine God's supernatural grace up to the point of rejecting its necessity. In this regard, we see Augustine condemning in Pelagianism the same ideas that Kant sustains.[50] While the philosophy of the cross,

---

49. "True religion consists not in knowing and confessing what God does, or may already have done, for our salvation, but in ourselves doing what must be done in order to make ourselves worthy of this benefit. Indispensably incumbent pursuits and avoidances can be those actions only that do in themselves possess an undoubted unconditioned worth, which can consequently alone render us acceptable to God, and whereof the practical necessity is self-evident to every man, and fully certain, quite apart from any Scripturary doctrines." Kant, *Religion*, Book 3, Second Part, 176,

50. ". . . he spoke of our *'meriting the divine grace by doing the will of God,'* in the sense that grace is added to those who believe and lead godly lives, whereby they may boldly withstand the tempter; whereas their very first reception of grace was, that they might do the will of God. Lest, then, he make such a rejoinder, consider some other words of his on this subject: *'The man,'* says he, *'who hastens to the Lord, and desires to be directed by Him, that is, who makes his own will depend upon God's, who moreover cleaves so closely to the Lord as to become (as the apostle says) 'one spirit' with Him (1 Cor 6:17) does all this by nothing else than by his freedom of will.'* Observe how great a result he has here stated to be accomplished only by our freedom of will; and how, in fact, he supposes us to cleave to God without the help of God: for such is the force of his words, *'by nothing else than by his own freedom of will.'* So that, after we have cleaved to the Lord without His help, we even then, because of such adhesion of our own, deserve to be assisted. For he goes on to say: *'Whosoever makes a right use of this* (that is, rightly uses his freedom of will), *does so entirely surrender himself to God, and does so completely mortify his own will, that he is able to say with the apostle, 'Nevertheless it is already not I that live, but Christ lives in me'* (Gal 2:20); and *'He places his heart in the hand of God, so that He turns it wherever He wills'* (Prov 21:1) . . . according to this writer's foolish opinion, however great the help may be, we deserve it all at the moment

according to Luther, presupposes a Christian religion where God sovereignly declares legally righteous and gradually makes ethically holy those whom he has eternally chosen to salvation, Pelagianism sees a religion where man autonomously restores himself to virtue and, therefore, where he makes himself worthy of God's favor. We see how well Kant's religion fits with the latter of these two diametrically opposed conceptions.

Consequently, we have in Kant also a Pelagian view of righteousness and justification. According to the philosophy of the cross, God's elect are declared legally righteous on the basis of the perfect atonement accomplished by Christ at the cross. This is theologically called "justification." What is usually called "sanctification" always flows from justification. It consists in an improvement in the ways of righteousness. Sanctification, however, never precedes justification. That is, good works do not produce righteousness, but true righteousness produces good works. For Kant, on the contrary, justification is founded on man's autonomous work of auto-sanctification, and true righteousness is autonomously achieved through the spontaneous exercise of the will in welcoming good maxims.[51] We have here a form of Pelagianism pushed to its extreme. This is no misrepresentation of Kant's position. In fact, we can read how, in several places, Augustine rebukes the Pelagians for implying, and sometimes explicitly

---

when, without any assistance beyond the liberty of our will, we hasten to the Lord, desire His guidance and direction, suspend our own will entirely on His, and by close adherence to Him become one spirit with Him. Now all these vast courses of goodness we (according to him) accomplish, forsooth, simply by the freedom of our own free will; and by reason of such antecedent merits we so secure His grace, that He turns our heart which way soever He pleases. . .' Augustine, *On the Grace of Christ and on Original Sin*, 22.24.

51. "Practically, where we do not investigate the physical constitution of the will of nature, but consider morally what is first to be done in regulating our free use of choice, viz. whether we are to begin with believing what God has done on our behalf, or should set forthwith about doing what we have to do in order to make ourselves worthy of it (whereinsoever this gift of the Divine Benignity may consist), then, questionless, the latter alternative must be adopted. To assume the first pre-requisite of our salvation, viz. a belief in vicarious satisfaction, is necessary nationally only, i.e. for a theoretical behoof, we cannot otherwise depicture to ourselves expurgation; the latter element, however, is practically necessary, and purely moral. This certain we can never hope to become partakers in the benefit of a foreign satisfactory merit, and so of eternal salvation, unless we qualify ourselves for such a blessing by unremittingly endeavouring to discharge all the offices of humanity; the performance of which duties must spring from our own effort, and not from any foreign influence whereby we are entirely passive. Again, because the ethical behest is unconditional, it follows of necessity that mankind must lay down, as a ground-work from which all faith must rise, this maxim, viz. that reformation of life is the supreme condition, apart from which there can be no room for any saving faith." Kant, *Religion*, Book 3, First Part, 7, 152–154,

expressing, a doctrine of autonomous righteousness which is significantly similar to the one supported by the transcendental philosopher: man is capable of becoming righteous in God's eyes even without the imputed righteousness graciously received by faith in the cross of Christ.[52] Kant, with a terminology typical of his age and marked by his own philosophy, holds to the same conception of righteousness.

Finally, Kant's entirely man-centered philosophy of religion renders the cross largely unnecessary. As we have seen, Kant declares the expiatory redemption of the cross not primarily relevant for ethics and religion inasmuch as man has all that he needs in virtue of his practical reason and the knowledge of the law offered by his reason to his free will. The Pelagianism of Kant was already evident from the parallel we have just made between *Religion*, Book 3, First Part, 7, and the Pelagian teaching reported and refuted by Augustine in *On Nature and Grace*, 9.10. For Kant, the cross is not the key epistemological principle that points to man's ethical fallenness and his absolute need of God's enlightening and redeeming work.[53] The cross is rather nothing more than a perfect example of virtue, given to man in order to show him the way toward the discovery and practice of religion within the boundaries of pure reason, a way that may also require personal sacrifice.[54] Christ is not the incarnate Logos who has revealed himself in humility in order to put to nought the bondage of man's reason to sin and self-centeredness, but rather he is the ideal representative of that idea of

---

52. "But they say: '*He is not condemned; because the statement that all sinned in Adam, was not made because of the sin which is derived from one's birth, but because of imitation of him.*' If, therefore, Adam is said to be the author of all the sins which followed his own, because he was the first sinner of the human race, then how is it that Abel, rather than Christ, is not placed at the head of all the righteous, because he was the first righteous man? But I am not speaking of the case of an infant. I take the instance of a young man, or an old man, who has died in a region where he could not hear of the name of Christ. Well, could such a man have become righteous by nature and free will; or could he not? If they contend that he could, then see what it is to render the cross of Christ of none effect (1 Cor 1:1), to contend that any man without it, can be justified by the law of nature and the power of his will. We may here also say, then is Christ dead in vain (Gal 2:21) forasmuch as all might accomplish so much as this, even if He had never died; and if they should be unrighteous, they would be so because they wished to be, not because they were unable to be righteous." Augustine, *On Nature and Grace*, 9.10.

53. Kant, *Religion*, Book 2, Apotome 1, Section B, 77,

54. "He by his example threw open the portals of freedom to all who, like him, chose to die to whatever kept them fettered to this earthly life disadvantageously to their morality, and gathers from among mankind, under his authority, a peculiar people, zealous of good works, leaving, the meanwhile, those who prefer the servitude of immorality, to their moral chains." *Ibid.*, Book 2, Apotome 2, 101

God that is helpful to man's reason in matters of morality.[55] Consequently, the cross of Christ has nothing to do with an atoning sacrifice to satisfy the absolutely inflexible requirements of God's holiness and law. Therefore, the philosophy of the cross is rejected on the basis of a supposed incompatibility with reason and its related juridical theorizations.[56] And it is especially here that, in my opinion, Luther's philosophical thesis is confirmed by Kant. The Prussian philosopher sees in Christianity the natural religion of man's reason.[57] As we have seen, however, Kant's idea of "Christianity" consistently characterized by a utter Pelagian approach to theology, is entirely auto-soteriological and man-centered. In fact, the conceptual pillars of theology of Kant's philosophy of religion are no novelty at all. They are the pillars of Pelagian theology. And, as has been demonstrated from Luther's works, the German thinker uncompromisingly asserted, over a century before Kant's Pelagian religion of pure reason, that man's natural religion consists in either explicit Pelagianism or a form of it.

In addition to all this, Kant and Pelagius share a significantly similar conception of the divine being. We can say that the Prussian philosopher set forth a secularized Pelagian theology. We dare to affirm that Kant, as a true heir of Pelagianism, brought Pelagianism to its most logical conclusion. Pelagius, even though he maintained a certain doctrine of the personality of God, implicitly but clearly denied such personality to God, especially regarding his saving operation in the world.

> Pelagianism was the daughter of legalism; but when it itself conceived, it brought forth an essential deism . . . the divine law is looked upon as a collection of separate commandments, moral perfection as a simple complex of separate virtues, and a distinct value as a meritorious demand on divine approbation is ascribed to each good work or attainment in the exercise of piety. It was

55. "Through a practical faith in this son of God (figured as having taken upon him our nature), mankind may hope to become acceptable to God (and so to enter into everlasting bliss), i.e. he who is conscious of such moral sentiments within, as enable him to believe and to place in himself a well-grounded trust, that he could, under any similar temptations and griefs (considered as the test and touchstone of the genuineness of that idea), ad here unchangeably to the archetype of humanity, and remain true to the exemplar by a steady following of his footsteps such a person, I say, and he alone, is entitled to look upon himself as one who may be an object not unworthy of the Divine complacency." *Ibid*, Book 2, Apotome 2, Section A, 74.

56. "Neither can this primordial guilt, antecedent to any good ever done by man (styled in the former book the radical evil of Human Nature), be taken away by any other person, so far as all our notices of the law of nature and reason reach." *Ibid.*, Book 2, Apotome 2, Section C, 88,

57. *Ibid.*, Book 4, Apotome 1, Section 1, 203–217.

because this was essentially his point that Pelagius could regard man's powers as sufficient to the attainment to sanctity—nay, that he could even assert it to be possible for a man to do more than was required of him. But this involved an essential deistic conception of man's relations to his Maker. God had endowed His creature with a capacity (*possibilitas*) or ability (*posse*) for action, and it was for him to use it. Man was thus a machine, which, just because it was well made, needed no Divine interference for its right working; and the Creator, having once framed him, and endowed him with *posse*, henceforth leaves the *velle* and the *esse* to him.[58]

Even though he belongs to the same philosophical group as Pelagius with respect to ethics and theology, Kant does not intend to maintain, nor does he judge necessary, the doctrine of a personal God. In this sense, Kant is more coherent than Pelagius himself because, as Warfield already explained, if man is properly equipped with auto-soteriological power and if grace is merely the knowledge of the moral law, this means that the illuminating and regenerating work of a personal God is ultimately not necessary.

Kant's philosophy of religion is diametrically opposed to Luther's Augustinian philosophy of the cross. It has already been pointed out that Luther himself would not be surprised. In his intellectual context, Luther already saw the rise of that theoretical attitude to ethics and theology which, according to him, hides ethical presuppositions under the cloak of supposed rational objectivity: "reason does not know nor understand the magnitude of divine mercy or how it is and how effective faith is . . . For they do not believe that incredible magnitude of God's power and mercy beyond all mercy. He who is righteous is willing to concede this, but he who is not righteous wants to consider himself righteous."[59] Therefore, we conclude that, from a Lutheran perspective, Kant's approach is philosophically Aristotelian, while the content and the conclusions of his approach are theologically Pelagian. In fact, on the one hand, Luther claimed that any attempt to judge religion according to mere reason always results in Pelagianism or in a form of Pelagianism. On the other hand, Kant's attempt to judge religion according to mere reason results in a distinctive Pelagian theology. If Kant has not proved Luther's thesis, it seems that he made no contribution whatsoever in order to disprove the claim of the German theologian.

58. Warfield, "Augustine and the Pelagian Controversy," 291.
59. Luther. Quoted in Althaus, *Luther*, 69.

However, Luther's philosophical thesis is not always so plainly demonstrated as it is in Kant's Pelagian theology. Kant, after all, displays in his
works a philosophy of religion marked by a explicit deism and a manifestly
auto-soteriological theology, two elements that are distinctively Pelagian.
What would we conclude if we analyzed a thinker who, between Luther's
teaching of moral necessity and Kant's ethical theology of absolute freedom, opts for a position that seeks to find a ground of compatibility between necessity and liberty? Do we have here the same outcomes if we
compare his philosophy of the will with the philosophy of the cross? We
will engage in this comparison, using Gottfried Wilhelm von Leibniz as an
excellent candidate who will help us in the third step of our philosophical
analysis. His *Theodicy* offers a condensed but at the same time detailed
exposition of what one of the greatest exponents of modern thought has to
tell us regarding the Lutheran thesis in which we are currently interested.

Leibniz's *Theodicy*

*It remains absurd to reason's judgement that God . . . should require
of "free-will" impossibilities . . . It is along this line that reason storms
and contends, in order to clear God of blame, and to vindicate His
justice and goodness!*[60]

We now discuss the results of Leibniz's philosophy of religion, i.e., we
examine whether the philosophical thesis of Luther is demonstrated also
in the teaching of Leibniz concerning free will, virtue, righteousness, and
the cross. His *Theodicy* is an ideal place to focus our attention. This work
is the *summa* of the thought of Leibniz, in which he discusses in depth the
topics which are the objects or our analysis. *Theodicy* intends to find the
definitive answer to the issues of the doctrine of God, the freedom of man,
and the problem of evil. As is typical of Leibniz in all of his work, the rationalistic philosopher aims to offer a strictly logical philosophical system
capable of answering questions and objections. Armed with the infallible
rules of analytics, Leibniz attempts to present a philosophical theology
which is the natural result of the agreement between faith and reason.
Furthermore, Leibniz, like Kant, though in a different way, claimed that
his theological conclusions were the result of the objective philosophizing
of reason, and that such reasoning is in accordance with faith. With this

60. Luther, *The Bondage of the Will*, 201–202.

is meant that in Leibniz, as in Kant, reason has a theoretical and practical priority over faith, where the term "faith" also includes the data of revelation. However, we will see that also in the case of Leibniz, for whom there seems to be more room than in Kant for the supernatural operation of a personal God, the result is an auto-soteriological religion where the ethical regeneration of man depends finally on the exercise of free will and autonomous virtuous morality. Therefore, also the theology of Leibniz's philosophy of religion is, from Luther's point of view, a theology of glory. It is here argued that, as for Kant, the conclusions of Leibniz's position are also a confirmation of Luther's thesis.

As has been our custom so far, we start with anthropology. The freedom of the will is for Leibniz an absolutely necessary concept, which is incompatible with any kind of strict necessity, both natural and moral. Leibniz does not make any precise distinction between natural necessity and moral necessity but, like Kant, he often seems to overlap the two concepts. For him, any kind of necessity would rule out liberty. If liberty were suppressed, Leibniz argues, spontaneity would also be eliminated. Without spontaneity of action, there is no ground for moral blame and praise, or for legal condemnation or absolution. Therefore, man has free will.[61] Before continuing our analysis, for those same theoretical reasons that have been explained several times, it will be necessary to mention Leibniz's treatment of the relationship between the doctrine of free will and the teaching of original sin.[62]

Leibniz, like Kant and Pelagius, needs to diminish the ethical and epistemological consequences of original sin in order to set forth his conception of the will. For Leibniz, a completely pervasive fallenness would imply a moral necessity that would be incompatible with his definition of liberty.[63] Therefore, he feels compelled to conclude that "there remains still

---

61. Leibniz, *Theodicy*, Part One, 1–2.

62. It has to be clarified that in the following analysis I am focusing exclusively on Leibniz's *theology*. On the philosophical side, Leibniz is a compatibilist, with a view of the faculty of the will similar to that of Jonathan Edwards (1703–1758), who with Augustine and Luther believed in the absolute necessity of grace. However, "on the theological side . . . Leibniz comes down squarely on the libertarian side." Murray, "Spontaneity and Freedom in Leibniz," 214. I am currently studying Edwards' and Leibniz's respective philosophies of the will in my doctoral thesis.

63. "The original corruption of the human race, coming from the first sin, appears to us to have imposed a natural necessity to sin without the succour of divine grace: but necessity being incompatible with punishment, it will be inferred that a sufficient grace ought to have been given to all men." Leibniz, *Theodicy*, Preface, 59.

a certain freedom after the fall."[64] Man is not in bondage to sin, as Luther
wrongly claimed, because a slave is still able to act freely, even though his
sphere of action is restrained.[65] Even though man is partially free, Leibniz seems at first glance to conclude a certain ethical corruption of man's
will in order to try to satisfy his more orthodox readers. However, this
understanding of his teaching is only apparent. In fact, Leibniz explicitly
asserts that "free will tends towards good, and if it meets with evil it is
by accident."[66] We have in Leibniz, as in Pelagianism, a doctrine of the
freedom of the will where the will is able to choose neutrally between good
and evil, so that the ethical depravity of man is far from being a necessity. On the contrary, man's will can defeat sinfulness even without God's
supernatural aid: "our corruption is not altogether invincible . . . we do
not necessarily sin even when we are under the bondage of sin."[67] This is
because, for the rationalist philosopher, sin does not have a primarily ethical nature. Rather, sin is an epistemological mistake, a logical fallacy. This
merely formal mistake occurs when man does not produce coherent and
ordered argumentations because he prefers to allow his syllogising to be
influenced by biases and disordered passions.[68] Thus, the restoration of the
good will has little to do with a spiritual regeneration, but it is rather the
re-education of the will to follow the correct procedures of reason: "God
has given to these creatures the art of always making good use of their
free will, for the natural light of reason is this art."[69] Ethical errors do not
occur because of a inner moral corruption of man's nature, but because
of a sort of intellectual laziness in not following in practice what correct
reason presents to man's will: "One must admit that there is always within
us enough power over our will, but we do not always bethink ourselves of
employing it."[70] Therefore, man's reason as well as his will, as intended by
Leibniz, are only superficially affected by man's fall into sin. In the world
of man, there is definitely more goodness than wickedness. The anthropological theology of thinkers like Augustine, Luther, and Calvin is not really

64. *Ibid.*, Part Three, 277.
65. *Ibid.*, Part Three, 279.
66. *Ibid.*, Part Two, 154.
67. *Ibid.*, Part Three, 279.
68. *Ibid.*, Preliminary Dissertation, 62.
69. *Ibid.*, Part Two, 120.
70. *Ibid.*, Part Three, 327.

the coherent conclusions of Christian presuppositions, but is rather the result of the gloomy theological positions of misanthropic personalities.[71]

In the Leibnizian system, as in every other system without exception, a certain presupposed anthropology results in a specific teaching of virtue and righteousness. We have seen that in the theological anthropology of Luther and Augustine, man's fallen will desperately needs the aid of supernatural enlightenment and regeneration in order to be restored to true righteousness, with the consequent possibility of a good virtuous life. In Leibniz, none of this is found, nor is it considered necessary. As for Pelagius and Kant in their Aristotelian approach to theology, so also for Leibniz, virtue and virtuousness are achieved autonomously by that moral exercise in which mankind is naturally able to engage: "I consider it unnecessary to say that all the virtues of the pagans were false or that all their actions were sins."[72] It is not a coincidence that Leibniz himself admits his conscious departure from Augustinianism and, consequently, from Luther: "this corruption of unregenerate man is, it must be added, no hindrance to his possession of true moral virtues and his performance of good actions in his civic life, *actions which spring from a good principle, without any evil intention and without mixture of actual sin.* Wherein I hope I shall be forgiven, if I have dared to diverge from the opinion of St. Augustine: he was doubtless a great man, of admirable intelligence, but inclined sometimes, as it seems, to exaggerate things, above all in the heat of his controversies."[73] In his criticism of Augustine, Leibniz, as the theological adversaries of Augustine and Luther did, accuses the African thinker of disparaging God's creation and providence: "It is nevertheless true that also on that point men in general exaggerate things, and that even some theologians disparage man so much that they wrong the providence of the Author of mankind. That is why I am not in favour of those who thought to do great honour to our religion by saying that the virtues of

71. "I am far from agreeing with him there, and I think that in reality, properly speaking, there is incomparably more moral good than moral evil in rational creatures; and of these we have knowledge of but few. This evil is not even so great in men as it is declared to be. It is only people of a malicious disposition or those who have become somewhat misanthropic through misfortunes, like Lucian's Timon, who find wickedness everywhere, and who poison the best actions by the interpretations they give to them. I speak of those who do it in all seriousness, to draw thence evil conclusions, by which their conduct is tainted; for there are some who only do it to show off their own acumen." *Ibid.*, Part Second, 220.

72. *Ibid.*, Part Three, 283.

73. *Ibid.*, Preface. Emphasis added.

the pagans were only *splendida peccata*,[74] splendid vices. It is a sally of St. Augustine's which has no foundation in holy Scripture, and which offends reason."[75] It is true that Leibniz often mentions God's supernatural grace as an aid to man's virtue. However, this grace is not the absolutely free and sovereignly irresistible grace taught by Augustine and Luther, but is rather a potential help that man must accept intellectually and practically, and that he can even reject. God's grace is, therefore, ultimately dependent on man's autonomous decision: "I would be rather on the side of those who grant to all men a grace sufficient to draw them away from evil, provided they have a sufficient tendency to profit by this succour, and not to reject it voluntarily."[76]

On the basis of this doctrine of virtue, grounded in the aforementioned conception of the will, Leibniz conceives also righteousness according to Pelagian criteria. As we have seen, for Luther's Augustinian philosophy of the cross, the requirements of God's law are so high and perfect that God himself, in light of man's impossibility to meet them, sent his own Word in the flesh legally to satisfy those requirements, with consequent righteousness for those who believe. However, this moral inability in which mankind has willingly and consciously plunged himself is very far from Leibniz's conception. The atoning sacrifice of Christ is not viewed as absolutely necessary, and righteousness consists in mere external commitment to the law carried out according to man's best morality: "it appears more reasonable and more fitting to say that obedience to God's precepts is always *possible*, even for the unregenerate."[77] In order to defend the power that man has to fulfill God's legal requirements, Leibniz must

74. Leibniz does not give any reference. This is because this is not a verbatim quote, but it is a motto traditionally attributed to Augustine's theology. This idea may easily be found in the works of the bishop of Hippo. See, for example, the following passage: "The virtues which it seems to itself to possess, and by which it restrains the body and the vices that it may obtain and keep what it desires, are *rather vices than virtues so long as there is no reference to God in the matter.* For although some suppose that virtues which have a reference only to themselves, and are desired only on their own account, are yet true and genuine virtues, the fact is that *even then they are inflated with pride, and are therefore to be reckoned vices rather than virtues.* For as that which gives life to the flesh is not derived from flesh, but is above it, so that which gives blessed life to man is not derived from man, but is something above him; and what I say of man is true of every celestial power and virtue whatsoever." Augustine, *The City of God*, 19.25.

75. Leibniz, *Theodicy*, Part Three, 259.

76. *Ibid.*, Part One, 95.

77. *Ibid.*, Part Three, 280. "Unregenerate" is a common term of Christian theology that indicates those individuals who have not been regenerated from their sinfulness by God's grace and who, therefore, remain in a state of fallenness.

on the one hand exalt the power of man's will[78] and, on the other hand, diminish the strictness of God's law,[79] as we have already seen in Kant and Pelagius. It follows that also in Leibniz's philosophy of religion we observe the overlapping of sanctification and justification. Righteousness flows from good works, rather than good works requiring righteousness: "God only pardons those who become better."[80]

In light of Leibniz's auto-soteriological theology, it is not surprising that the cross of Christ is hardly mentioned in his vast *Theodicy*. Even though Jesus Christ is the "divine founder of the purest and most enlightened religion,"[81] his cross is not the central epistemological principle that displays ethics, intended as both man's ethical nature and man's ethical obligations. In establishing the doctrine of man's will, the teaching on virtue, righteousness, and enlightenment, the cross is not central. In fact, both the anthropology of Leibniz and his doctrine of self-achievable redemption and enlightenment witness against the absolute necessity of the cross of Christ as intended in the philosophy of the cross. This was already clear from the fact that Leibniz views sin as merely epistemological in nature: "Right reason is a linking together of truths, corrupt reason is mixed with prejudices and passions. And in order to discriminate between the two, one need but proceed in good order, admit no thesis without proof, and admit no proof unless it be in proper form, according to the commonest rules of logic."[82] Since sinfulness has mostly, if not exclusively, an intellectual essence which has not essentially corrupted man's nature, the atoning cross of the incarnate Logos is not strictly necessary. This is because man is able in detect this rational fallenness and autonomously to recover from it. Moreover, even in the case where a person is not intellectually well equipped, God is at peace with the best efforts that he is able to accomplish on the basis of his natural abilities.[83] The cross becomes something secondary, and the incarnation of the Logos which is the subject of philosophical investigation is not foundational because man's redemption,

78. *Ivi.*

79. *Ibid.*, Part Three 283.

80. *Ibid.*, Part Two, 133.

81. *Ibid.*, Preface.

82. *Ibid.*, Preliminary Dissertation, 62.

83. "It will be possible to say that God will give that knowledge to all those who do, humanly speaking, that which in them lies, even though God must needs give it by a miracle." *Ibid.*, Part One, 98. See also Part One, 95.

which mainly corresponds with a mere rational enlightenment, is spontaneously and autonomously carried out by man himself.[84]

It is true that the theological corollaries of the philosophy of Leibniz
are somewhat different from those of Kant. In fact, Kant's theology is manifestly Pelagian. As we have seen, according to Kant, the entirety of man's
enlightenment and redemption is described in terms of a mere adaptation
of the will to the legal dictates of reason and, therefore, as in Pelagianism,
we have in Kant a purely auto-soteriological religion. Leibniz, however,
sometimes appears to teach something slightly different. For him, only the
beginning of faith and faith itself, or at least the desire of it, is produced
by man, and God's help follows. Therefore, if it could be argued that we do
not have explicit Pelagianism in Leibniz's theology, we can still argue that
his position is characterized by semi-Pelagianism.[85] However, according
to the Augustinian philosophy of the cross expressed by Luther, this variation makes very little difference. It has already been shown that, according
to Luther, both Pelagianism and Semi-Pelagianism, in all their variations,
are nothing but different forms of the antithetical counterpart of Christianity represented in the revelatory event of the cross. Also Augustine,
coherently with his theology of absolute grace, is uncompromising in his
approach to this issue. Already in his *Letters* 217, Augustine treated Semi-
Pelagianism "as necessarily implying the basal idea of Pelagianism."[86] In
fact, this letter shows us that Augustine attempted to demonstrate how the
error of semi-Pelagianism, with its teaching of man's inherent faith and
ability autonomously to exercise it, has essentially the same theological
nature as Pelagianism and it tends to Pelagianism. Moreover, this juxtapo-
sition seems to be implied throughout Augustine's confutation contained

84. "Etsi enim multi populi nunquam salutarem Christi doctrinam acceperint, nec
credibile sit praedicationem ejus apud omnes quibus defuit irritam futuram fuisse,
Christo ipso de Sodoma contrarium affirmante: non ideo tamen necesse est aut sal-
vari aliquem sine Christo , aut damnari, etsi praestitisset quicquid per naturam po-
test. Neque enim nobis omnes viae Dei exploratae sunt, neque scimus an non aliquid
extraordinaria ratione praestetur vel morituris. Pro certo enim tenendum est, etiam
Cornelii exemplo, si qui ponantur bene usi lumine quod accepere, eis datum iri lumen
quo indigent, quod nondum accepere, etiamsi in ipso mortis articulo dandum esset."
Leibniz, *Causa Dei Asserta per Iustitiam Eius*, 111.

85. For the similarities between the theology of Leibniz and semi-Pelagianism,
compare Leibniz's teaching with two of the letters of the most prominent exponents
of semi-Pelagianism, Prosper and Hilary, in *Letters* 225 and 226. To these two letters,
Augustine answered with his treatise on predestination and perseverance, traditionally
divided into two books, namely, *On The Predestination of the Saints* and *On the Gift of
Perseverance*.

86. Warfield, "Augustine and the Pelagian Controversy," 389.

in his final works on the Semi-Pelagian controversy.[87] Also for Augustine, as we have seen for Luther, to ascribe both the entirety or a small part of man's redemption to himself means to reject the philosophy of the cross altogether. From the perspective of the philosophy of the cross, the semi-Pelagianism that Leibniz appears to embrace is nothing but a sophisticated version of Pelagianism. This is because the work of man's ethical and epistemological restoration does not belong to man as Kant and Pelagianism assert, nor partially to man as Leibniz and Semi-Pelagianism claim, but entirely to God. The theology of Leibniz, therefore, confirms Luther's thesis: any attempt to develop a theology of mere reason and not of revelation, or at least where reason is the judge of revelation and not the contrary, always results in Pelagianism or in one of its expressions.

Conclusions

The identification of the Augustinianism of Luther's *Heidelberg Disputation*, the *manifesto* of Luther's theology, has been instrumental in showing that the Lutheran philosophy of the cross is not entirely novel. This position has its origin in the ancient period, and in particular in Augustine, the greatest of the church fathers and one of the greatest Christian philosophers. In addition to this, we have seen that the intention of the German reformer in writing the disputation that he publically discussed at Heidelberg was to demonstrate that his message was a permissible development of Augustinianism in light of the theological and intellectual circumstances of his day. It is the conviction of the present writer that the continuity between Augustine's theology of absolute grace and Luther's theology of the cross is undeniable. In order to demonstrate this assertion, the research has conducted a close comparative reading of the Augustinian and Lutheran texts, which has demonstrated the agreement of Luther and Augustine on the issues of free will, virtue, righteousness and the cross. This means that Luther was right to call Augustine an authority in support of his position, and that the message of the German finds its theoretical justification in Augustine. This was the first step of the present research which has required extensive theological discussion.

However, the theological nature of the first part of the present work was instrumental in the discussion of the second part, in which we have deduced from the paradoxes of the *Heidelberg Disputation* the

---

87. *On Grace and Free Will, On Rebuke and Grace, On the Predestination of the Saints*, and *On the Gift of Perseverance*.

philosophical thesis concerning the antitheticality of the philosophy of the cross. According to this concept, in theology and consequently in philosophy there are basically only two possibilities: a proper Christological conception, or some form of Pelagianism. Luther predicted that when reason works independently from the data of revelation, or when these data are improperly handled, the outcome is always an auto-soteriological form of religion. In their philosophies, Kant and Leibniz attempted to do exactly what Luther judged as erroneous, and consequently their philosophies of religion display the same features that Luther predicted. In fact, Kant and Leibniz aimed to establish, according to their own respective terms, a religion where "reason" either has the first place (Leibniz) or is essentially sovereign (Kant). Consequently, it has been shown how the theological outcomes of their philosophies of religion are those that Luther predicted. Kant and Leibniz have been shown to have the essential elements of Pelagianism and Semi-Pelagianism, respectively. In this way, through Kant and Leibniz, the research has attempted to prove Luther's philosophical prediction.

As far as the philosophical thesis itself is concerned, supported by the demonstration of the Augustinianism of Luther's philosophy of the cross, the present writer is convinced that the confirmation which this thesis receives from the philosophies of religion of Leibniz and Kant could foster interest in further study of the intellectual departure of mainstream philosophy from the ethics of Augustine and Luther, two of the main founders of western society. Augustine's philosophy represented a radical departure from the classical philosophical conception of virtue and, accordingly, from classical ethics. Luther, who we have seen is Augustinian, with his philosophy of the cross, gave voice to Augustine's theology of absolute grace and its related theological ethics. Thus, he developed and strengthened the Augustinian antithesis between secular and humanistic ethics and Christian revealed ethics. In addition to this, Luther foretold the modern departure from Augustinian ethics as a necessary departure from the philosophy of the cross. This departure is a result always produced by the philosophy of the cross. Kant's Pelagianism and Leibniz' Semi-Pelagianism are a clear proof of this departure.

As far as the modern age is concerned, it is here suggested that it is possible to continue the same analysis with other modern philosophers, such as, for example, Friedrich Schleiermacher and Søren Aabye Kierkegaard. In this case, the analysis would be dedicated to two thinkers who have a significantly different approach to religion than Kant and

Leibniz. It is true that Schleiermacher and Kierkegaard do not base their philosophical efforts on the concept of reason but rather on the "feeling of dependence" and "existence" or "becoming a Christian" respectively. Nevertheless, it is the conviction of the writer that also the theological conclusions of their theologies confirm the accuracy of the antitheticality of the cross. Moreover, we dare to assert that a study of the Pelagian origins of the mainstream philosophy of religion of the modern age may also prove the accuracy of the thesis of Luther discussed so far. But this is not the place to discuss this issue, and what has been said about Schleiermacher and Kierkegaard and the philosophy of religion of the modern age must remain a mere assertion, at least for the moment, and will have to be demonstrated elsewhere.

Alongside with what previously has been stated, the present research has conducted an analysis that may illumine further studies on the relationship between philosophy and ethical premises. It seems that the vast majority of modern thinkers fail to recognize the fact that, in order to philosophize, or even in order simply to think, some indemonstrable premises are necessary. These indemonstrable premises are the axioms on the basis of which the thinker builds his system. It is permissible, even necessary, to assume premises. However, it needs to be recognized that these premises are merely chosen, and not proved. To attribute rational objectivities to these premises at the very start of our philosophizing, as Kant seems to do several times, would appear to commit the logical fallacy of *petitio principi*, or "begging the question," that is, judging as true the conclusions that one wants to prove. In fact, the accuracy of one's premises must be judged at the end of the development of the system, according to the inner coherency and cohesion of the system itself, and not at the beginning of reasoning. Maybe it is also because of this methodological failure that "Kant, for example, the source of all contemporary philosophy, or at least the tunnel through which all modern ideas have passed, is unbearably self-contradictory."[88] In this regard, Luther assumes the most

---

88. Clark, *A Christian View of Man and Things*, 29. This is not the place to engage in a critical reading of Kant. However, considering the importance that the issue of the will has had in this research, we may mention Kant's position of the 'inscrutability' of the subjective ground of the maxim. By this the philosopher means the determinative motive of moral life, the foundation on which man determines the acts of his will, i.e., the maxims that pure reason suggests to him. For Kant, the first ground of a maxim must be in another maxim. This means that the ground of all maxims is a foundational, originating maxim. However, this foundational ground, being itself a maxim, needs another maxim as its ground, because all maxims are grounded in maxims, and not in nature. This is a great inconsistency to which Kant does not give a sufficient answer.

honest approach: he openly shows the ethical premises which he presupposes. He knows and acknowledges that his axioms are chosen, and his axioms are the axioms of revelation, contained in Scripture. It is on the basis of these premises of theological ethics that he builds both his theology and his philosophy.

In light of these considerations, and as it has already be noted, it may be said that Luther developed his philosophy of the cross also because he began to see that many of his colleagues were voluntarily or involuntarily hiding their chosen Pelagian and Aristotelian ethical presuppositions under the appearances of rational objectivity. Through the archetypal examples of Leibniz and Kant, it has been demonstrated that these two thinkers base their philosophy of religion on ethical axioms that are very close to Pelagian ethics and theology. Therefore, since Leibniz and Kant are so influential for the philosophy of the modern period, it can be argued that Luther's philosophical diagnosis of his own intellectual context can also be considered a prediction of the mainstream philosophy of religion of the Modern era. Luther's prophetical philosophical theses may be useful to justify the study of the history of philosophy from the point of view of the ethical presuppositions assumed by its main figures, a sort of ethical presuppositionalism. In this regard, the intuition of Luther and his ethical presuppositionalism can be beneficial to understand if, why, and how presupposed ethical premises constitute the preeminent element of the activity of philosophizing; if, why, and how presupposed ethics produces, guides and influences our philosophy or worldview; and how, why and which philosopher or philosophical school does not acknowledge the necessary moral axioms that he, she, or it assumes, premises without which philosophizing is impossible. In this regard, we could quote a rather unexpected thinker, considering the nature of this research. His words

---

Simply to assert that the principle is "inscrutable" is a rhetorical device. Rather, it would be more logical to say that such a concept of human nature is, rather than inscrutable, inconsistent. This is because it implies an irresolvable absurdity of a ground that goes backwards *in infinitum*. Moreover, Kant merely states that, if necessity is presupposed, imputation of evil or virtue becomes impossible. However, Kant does not make any sufficient distinction between moral necessity (where the will is conscious and consenting to an internal impulse) and natural necessity (where the will is opposed by an impulse external and contrary to its inclination). On the contrary, he dismisses every kind of necessity as natural necessity. It is enough to point to Jonathan Edwards, who answered several of Kant's points. Even though Edwards never read Kant's critical philosophy (he died when Kant was only 33 years old), his *Freedom of the Will* offers significant objections and solutions to several foundational points which will be adopted and developed later by the philosopher of Königsberg. See Edwards, *Freedom of the Will*, 171-194..

about the preeminence, or at least the essential role, of presupposed ethics appear to be in harmony with what has just been asserted.

> It has gradually become clear to me what every great philosophy up till now has consisted of—namely, the confession of its originator, and a species of involuntary and unconscious autobiography; and moreover that the moral (or immoral) purpose in every philosophy has constituted the true vital germ out of which the entire plant has always grown. Indeed, to understand how the abstrusest metaphysical assertions of a philosopher have been arrived at, it is always well (and wise) to first ask oneself: *What morality do they (or does he) aim at?* . . . In the philosopher there is absolutely nothing impersonal; and above all, his morality furnishes a decided and decisive testimony as to WHO HE IS—that is to say, in what order the deepest impulses of his nature stand to each other.[89]

Of course, it is almost unnecessary to say that the investigative question that Nietzsche directs to the category of philosophers is very well applicable to his own thought.

---

89. Nietzsche, *Beyond Good and Evil*, 1.6. Emphasis added.

BIBLIOGRAPHY

"Vulgate Bible." http://www.biblestudytools.com/vul/

Agostino, "Lo Spirito e la Lettera." http://www.augustinus.it/italiano/spirito_lettera/index2.htm

Althaus, Paul, *The Theology of Martin Luther*. Philadelphia, PA: Fortress Press, 1966.

Aristotle, "Nicomachean Ethics." http://classics.mit.edu/Aristotle/nicomachaen.html

Atkinson, James, *Martin Luther and the Birth of Protestantism*. London: Penguin Book, 1968.

Augustine, "Contra Iulianum haeresis Pelagianae defensorem libri sex." http://www.augustinus.it/latino/contro_giuliano/index.htm

———, "The Rule." http://www.augustinians.net/index.php?page=the-rule

Barone, Marco, "Agostino e l'Accademia Scettica nel *Contra Academicos*." BA Thesis, Università degli Studi di Napoli "Federico II," 2012.

Berkhof, Hendrik, *200 anni di teologia e filosofia*. Torino: Claudiana, 1992.

Beschin Giuseppe, et al. *Lutero e i linguaggi dell'Occidente*. Brescia: Morcelliana, 2002.

Boga, Sister M. Inez, ed., *The Fathers of the Church. Saint Augustine. The Retractions*. Washington, DC: The Catholic University of America, 1999.

Brown, Peter, *Augustine of Hippo*. London: Faber and Faber, 2000.

Burleigh, J. H. S., ed., *Augustine. Earlier Writings*. Louisville, KY: Westminster John Knox, 2006.

Buzzi, Franco, 'Introduzione.' In Martin Lutero, *La lettera ai Romani (1515–1516)*. Cinesello Balsamo: San Paolo, 1991.

Calvin, John, *Institutes of Christian Religion*. Peabody, MA: Hendrickson, 2008.

———. *The Bondage and the Liberation of the Will*. Grand Rapids, MI: Baker, 2002.

Cantor, Peter, "Verbum Abbreviatum." http://www.mlat.uzh.ch/download_pl/?lang=0&dir=/var/www/Corpus2_PL/&file=205_Petrus-Cantor_Verbum-abbreviatum.xml&xml=1

Clark, Gordon H., *A Christian View of Man and Things*. Unicoi, TN: The Trinity Foundation, 2005.

———. *Logic*. Unicoi, TN: The Trinity Foundation, 2004.

De Biase, Riccardo, *L'agostinismo di Martin Lutero tra peccato e predestinazione. Le radici medievali e moderne della "gettatezza" umana*. Napoli: Partagees, 2006.

Deferrari, Roy Joseph, ed., *The Fathers of the Church. Saint Augustine. Against Julian*. New York: Fathers of the Church, 1957.

Edwards, Jonathan, *The Works of Jonathan Edwards*. Vol. 1. *Freedom of the Will*. New Haven, CT: Yale University, 1957.

Ferrari, L. C., *The Conversions of Saint Augustine*. Villanova, PA: Villanova University, 1984.

Fitzgerald, Allan D., ed., *Augustine Trough the Ages. An Encyclopedia*. Grand Rapids, MI: Eerdmans, 1999.

Forde, Gerhard O., *On Being a Theologian of the Cross*. Grand Rapids, MI: Eerdmans, 1997.

Fredriksen, Paula, "Paul and Augustine: Conversion Narratives, Orthodox Traditions, and Retrospective Self." *Journal of Theological Studies* 37:3–4.

Gilson Étienne, *Introduzione allo studio di sant'Agostino*. Genova: Marietti, 2007.

Harnack, Adolf von, *History of Dogma*. Vol. 5. https://www.ccel.org/ccel/harnack/dogma6.i.html

Harrison, Carol, *Augustine. Christian Truth and Fractured Humanity*. Oxford: Oxford University Press, 2000.

———. *Rethinking Augustine's early theology. An Argument for Continuity*. Oxford: Oxford University Press, 2008.

J. J. O'Donnell, 'The Next Life of Augustine.' In *The Limits of Ancient Christianity: Essay in Late Antique Thought and Culture in Honor of R. A. Markus*, edited by W.E. Klingshirn and M. Vessey. Ann Arbor, MI: University of Michigan, 1999.

Kant, Immanuel, *Religion Within the Boundaries of Mere Reason*. Edinburgh: Thomas Clark, 1838. https://archive.org/details/religionwithinookantuoft

———. *The Conflict of the Faculties*. New York: Abaris, 1979.

Leibniz, Gottfried Wilhelm von, *Causa Dei Asserta per Iustitiam Eius*. Frankfurt: Caroli Josephi Bencard, 1719. https://books.google.co.uk/books?id=6O2cGGouHisC&printsec=frontcover&source=gbs_ge_summary_r&cad=0#v=onepage&q&f=false.

———. *Theodicy. Essays on the Goodness of God, the Freedom of Man and the Origin of Evil*. La Salle, IL: Open Court, 1996. https://ia801400.us.archive.org/29/items/theodicy17147gut/17147-h/17147-h.htm#page49

Lettieri, Gaetano, *L'altro Agostino. Ermeneutica e retorica della grazia dalla crisi alla metamorfosi del De Doctrina Christiana*. Brescia: Morcellina, 2001.

Levering, Matthew, *The Theology of Augustine: An Introductory Guide to His Most Important Works*. Grand Rapids, MI: Baker Academic, 2013.

Loewenich, Walther von, *Luther's Theology of the Cross*. Belfast: Christian Journal Limited, 1976.

Lombard, Peter, "Sententiarum Libri Quatuor." http://www.documentacatholicaomnia.eu/02m/1095–1160,_Petrus_Lombardus,_Sententiarum_Libri_Quatuor,_MLT.pdf

Lull, Timothy F., ed., *Martin Luther's Basic Theological Writings*. Minneapolis, MN: Fortress, 2005.

Luther, Martin, "An Open Letter on Translating." http://www.bible-researcher.com/luther01.html.

———. *Commentary on Galatians*. Grand Rapids, MI: Kregel, 1979.

———. *The Bondage of the Will*. Grand Rapids, MI: Revel–Baker, 2002.

Madec, Goulven, *La Patrie et la Voi*. Paris: Desclée, 1989.

Malatesta, Enrico, "La problematica linguistica nel *Contra Academicos* alla luce della filosofia del linguaggio contemporanea." *Metalogicon* 10, 2 (1997) 46–63.

———. "St. Augustine's Dialectic from the Modern Logic Standpoint. Logical Analysis of *Contra Academicos* 3.10.22–13.29." *Metalogicon* 8, 2 (1995) 91–120.

McGrath, Alister, *Luther's Theology of the Cross. Martin Luther's Theological Breakthrough*. Wiley-Blackwell, 2011.

Miegge, Giovanni, *Lutero. L'uomo e il pensiero fino alla dieta di Worms*. Torino: Claudiana, 2008.

Murray, Michael J, "Spontaneity and Freedom in Leibniz." In *Leibniz. Nature and Freedom*. Edited by Donald Rutherford and J. A. Cover, 194–216. Oxford: Oxford University, 2005.

Needham, N. R., *The triumph of grace. Augustine's writings on Salvation*. London: Sovereign Grace, 2005.

Nello Cipriani, "Le fonti cristiane della dottrina trinitaria nei primi Dialoghi di s. Agostino." *Augustinianim* 34 (1994) 253–312.

Nietzsche, Friedrich, *Beyond Good and Evil*. http://onlinebooks.library.upenn.edu/webbin/gutbook/lookup?num=4363.

Pani, Giancarlo, 'Introduzione.' In *Lezioni sulla lettera ai romani (1515–1516)*. Genova: Marietti, 1991–1992.

———. *Martin Lutero. Lezioni sulla Lettera ai Romani. I riferimenti ad Agostino. La giustificazione*. Roma: Agostiniane, 1983.

———. *Paolo, Agostino, Lutero: alle origini del mondo moderno*. Soveria Manelli: Rubettino, 2005.

Pauck, Wilhelm, ed., *Luther: Lectures on Romans*. Philadelphia, PA: Westminster, 1961.

Pintacuda, F. De Michelis, 'Introduzione.' In Martin Lutero, *Il servo arbitrio*. Torino: Claudiana, 1993.

Pontifex, Dom Mark, ed., *Ancient Christian Writers. Saint Augustine. The Problem of Free Choice*. New York: Newman Press, 1955.

Ramsey, Boniface and John E. Rotelle, eds., *The Works of Saint Augustine. Letters 211–270*. New York: New City, 2005.

Schaff, Philip, *History of the Christian Church. Vol. 3*. https://www.ccel.org/ccel/schaff/hcc3

———. ed., *Nicene and Post-Nicene Fathers, First Series, Vol. 1–5*. Buffalo: Christian Literature, 1887. http://www.newadvent.org/fathers/

Spaeth, Adolph, L.D. Reed, Henry Eyster Jacobs, eds., *Works of Martin Luther. Vol. 1*. Philadelphia, PA: A. J. Holman, 1915.

Spitz, Lewis William and Helmut T. Lehman, eds., *Luther's Works Volume 34. Career of the Reformer. IV*. St. Louis, MO: Concordia, 1960.

Stump, Eleonore and Norman Kretzmann, eds., *The Cambridge Companion to Augustine*. Cambridge; Cambridge University, 2006.

Warfield, B. B., "Augustine and the Pelagian Controversy." In B. B. Warfield, *Studies in Tertullian and Augustine*. New York: Oxford University, 1930.

Wood, Arthur Skevington, *Captive to the Word. Martin Luther: Doctor of Sacred Scripture*. Exeter: Paternoster, 1969.

Made in the USA
Coppell, TX
03 February 2021

49538552R00095